I0542864

IN THE AMERICAS

For Robert Bohm, the America we despair over and cower before is already a little behind. He walks the road of an exile in his own land, and his anger is the emanation of his love . . . *In the Americas* (is) the most serious, the most radical, the most visionary of all the books considered for . . . our prize for the year's best poetry volume by a new writer.
—From the Great Lakes Colleges Association (GLCA) Awards Committee

CLOSING THE HOTEL KITCHEN

Closing the Hotel Kitchen is a great and important work. Bohm's stunning language and brilliant poetics are a match for its vision. The impetus is nothing less than to be a midwife of a whole new way to write.
—Sharon Doubiago, author of the classic *Hard Country* and many other poetry books, short story collections and memoirs

Robert Bohm's *Closing the Hotel Kitchen* is full of a quiet anger that burns like white phosphorous. There is no turning away from these poems and no forgiveness. They relentlessly catch us off guard and the voices hold us--tugging at our sleeves and forcing us and forcing us to see their awful truths. These are essential poems of our moment.
—Gerald McCarthy, author of *Trouble Light*, *The Doorway in the Wall*, other poetry volumes and a forthcoming memoir

PRAISE FROM INDIA FOR WHAT THE BIRD TATTOO HIDES

Bohm's book is a poetry of witness at its best. His poems on India are completely free from the exoticizing and mystifying gaze of too many non-Indian writers. India here is no wonderland of sages and snake charmers. This poet's mind is keyed to the sounds, colours, textures and feelings of everyday India. For him "seeing is prayer-like. And dangerous depending on whose eyes."
—K.Satchidanandan, one of India's foremost poets, has published more than 20 poetry volumes and his work has been translated into 17 languages

Nightmares
That Leave Grease Stains
On Psych Ward Walls

Poems on endless war

Robert Bohm

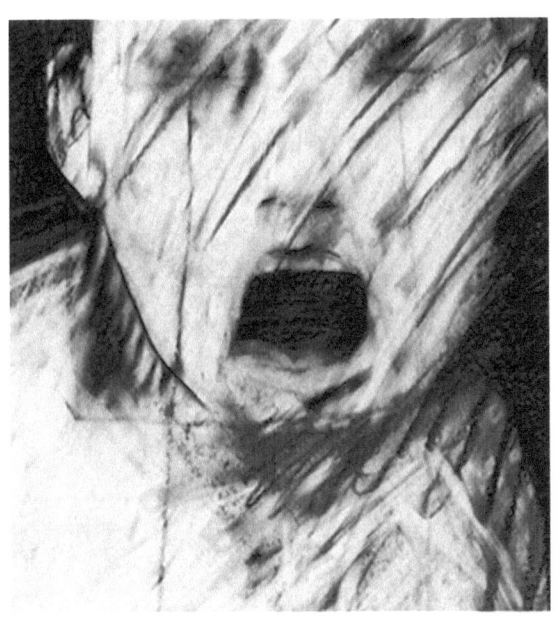

SPUYTEN DUYVIL

NEW YORK CITY

© 2023 Robert Bohm
ISBN 978-1-959556-16-9
The cover image is artist Rick Bartow's graphite drawing, 'Things You Know But Cannot
Explain.' It is used here with permission from the Bartow Trust.

Library of Congress Cataloging-in-Publication Data

Names: Bohm, Robert, author.
Title: Nightmares that leave grease stains on psych ward walls : poems on
    endless war / Robert Bohm.
Description: New York : Spuyten Duyvil, [2023]
Identifiers: LCCN 2023000179 | ISBN 9781959556169 (paperback)
Subjects: LCSH: Post-traumatic stress disorder--Poetry. | LCGFT: Poetry.
Classification: LCC PS3552.O52 N54 2023 | DDC 811/.54--dc23/eng/20230113
LC record available at https://lccn.loc.gov/2023000179

For Gerald McCarthy,
Marine Vietnam veteran, friend & a poet whose work inspires me.
Without his support & advice,
this book would not have been written.

Also, for all those others,
soldiers, spouses, children, parents, refugees,
citizens & so-called enemies,
who in one way or another have been caught
in the crosshairs of the US's ongoing wars.

And for Suman,
always my first reader,
always struggling to right society's wrongs,
always my wife, friend, lover, teacher.

". . . this is not somewhere else but here,
our country moving closer to its own truth and dread,
its own ways of making people disappear."
—Adrienne Rich

*

"The object of waging a war is always to be in a better position
in which to wage another."
—George Orwell

*

"Quiet. No one hears
No one feels the tears
of multitudes."
—Sonia Sanchez

CONTENTS

Prologue

When did I return

NIGHTMARES
THAT LEAVE GREASE STAINS
ON PSYCH WARD WALLS

Prologue

WHICH STORM IS THIS?

A torrent sweeps
in sheets across the yard. Once again
the monsoon has
arrived.
We're here its whipping winds announce
as they lash paddies
to my right while billowing
in front of me through trees
where snipers wait while I hide
in a trench with water at the bottom. Shivering
I pray to a future me
in a home in which I've lived for decades
but still don't recognize because
pineapple groves and mangrove swamps block
my view no matter from what
angle I gaze.
The rain's unceasing, the muddy water
at the trench's bottom rises to my nose, after which
I crawl out, slithering forward, belly-down
in a panic, an infinity
of back yards all around me.
Lightning flashes above a toolshed, then thunder explodes
as my wife, kneeling
next to me, pleads
It's time honey,
please stop freaking me out,
you gotta come inside.

When did I return

Aaron's tales

Flying at twelve hundred feet, the chopper's rotors
made a thumping sound
as they cut the air
while six of us sat in canvas seats
by the cargo doors.

In spite of the noise, I heard
his voice—low, almost trance-like,
a bedtime story. As
he spoke, I saw him step over
a horseshoe crab while the bay tongued
his feet. How clear
it all was—seaweed
scattered on sand here and there,
the tide
going out.

Before long the seasons
changed. He took us then
for a trek along the same shore in a snowfall so heavy
we could barely see the water.
There's a duck blind up ahead, he muttered.
Although we didn't know where we were going
we didn't care.
Following him, heads bent down, we tramped
into the wind.

Soon the Huey landed at the LZ. Dust
swarmed all around us, a storm
of thoughts that wouldn't cohere.

SOON ENOUGH I'M TAKING IT IN STRIDE

for Kathrine Taylor

Even after it was dead, I beat the snake
with the shovel as night came on.
I felt better then.

Like the others, I'm a carrier
of the sacred. I bring it with me
as we trek in country. Can you
smell it? It's in my fatigues, the scent
of incense from huts you've never seen.
Like God, the huts
light up the world, as they burn behind us.

Tonight opium shows me the fuckhole
 in the bamboo sapling.
Hump me skinny lady so I can dump
 my riddles into you, I think.
Unimpressed, she remains bamboo.

In the morning, the unknown's
 mercenaries, we go on patrol.
Whatever I'm supposed to find in front of me
is behind.
Turning around, I locate nothing
in the egret's shadow.
Like the Holy Ghost, no VC
moves loudly enough to be noticed.

Alone with my native tongue, I must unlearn
what it once claimed to know
but didn't.
But first I must remember
which sound means *grunt*, which *groan*.

FRAGMENTS OF SOMETHING

Look. Over there. A corpse
from 2nd Platoon. Note how
it stretches the space around it
toward it, making trees, paddies, APCs
& grunts unable to free themselves
from its pull. The corpse
holds us in its spell
like a demonic mommy about to eat
her kids.

Hypnotized, we watch how this freak
of nature, this atrocity
born of panic's viscera, rises
to its feet, wielding a flamethrower that leaves
smoldering portents everywhere—
even the air's on fire,
our minds burnt to a crisp.

Morning. I stand in my boxers, staring
out the Motel 6 window into heavy rain
up north, in Deerfield.
Across the road, the Mekong River winds across
the landscape, grass and trees vivid green.
I shiver a bit as the thatched roof leaks
and a waterbuffalo wanders at the parking lot's edge
in the downpour.
I can't drag myself from the window,
can't let go of my M16.

At a certain point, the soul grows silent. Homeless
it goes dumpster-diving, hunting

slender sentences dripping with marinara sauce

syllables made from the sound of growing mold

random insights the size of chicken pellets

vegetable scraps shaped like question marks and commas—anything

with which to assemble
new stories to tell
on the corner of Front and Walnut Streets
as folks depart the train station, hands
clasped over their ears.

Since Tonkin . . . Then after, when . . .
The point is, the pills change, but the swallowing doesn't.
The stints in the hospital change, but the corridors don't.
No matter the year, when the nurse looks around stunned,
she's on the hunt. For you. *Oh, there you are!* she yells, spying you
strapped to a table, in the midst of a spasm.
The artillery's loud. Tripwires everywhere. BOOM
something goes up in smoke.
Are you ok? someone asks.
This is your moment. Don't answer. Don't smile. Not
at the nurse, not

at the jury, not at the guy prosecuting you.
You spasm again.
This time you hide in a hole and don't come out.
When the time's right, you'll make your move.
But when'll that be, I don't know. It's your, not my, riddle to solve.

I awaken, floating on the Mekong. It bends
and unbends. Mind
strays here, then there.

Wherever it flows, I go. Whenever
it drowns me, I drown.
I love
the downward tow.

Before going under,
I read what the clouds hide. Afterwards
further down
I listen to the sound of fish gills flapping
against cold scales. Interpreting
the signs, I find
my way. Later
having exited the water, I camp
in a landfill for the night.
Before sleep
I disassemble, reassemble my M16.
Many possibilities await me now.

Don't ask me who I am.
Ask who I was *meant* to be.

Random mind wanderings

Good day, bad day? Can't say. Earlier, while on a jungle march, imagined myself trudging through New York's midtown garment district. In the daydream, I spotted OD'd rock 'n' roll singers' skins hanging from clothing racks near a sign that blared —

Big sale wear your favorite songster's epidermis get it cheap!

When my stupid fantasy ended, I stopped thinking. Saw trail, became trail. Nothing else. Only *going.*

Grunts behind & ahead. All *going.*

In base camp sunlight, I thought of Jamila from the Bronx. Her bullet scar. The scar's from an accident when she was fifteen. Her grandma tried to kill a pigeon with a pistol and the bullet ricocheted off a cement wall and hit Jamila above the right elbow. These days she squats in Co-Op City with two aunts and her Uncle Johnny. Those who know her say she's living proof a person can love Jesus and Fidel Castro simultaneously.

Her cousin Elesio from our platoon told me this . . . Me? I never met her.

Three nights ago, a dream. In it mom wheelchaired at top speed into my room as if she was zooming toward the answer to the $64,000 Question on TV. Hollering, she woke me up—*Do you know what's happening? Do you know?* I didn't have the faintest idea what she was blabbing about. Still, I muttered, *Of course I know.* Dead three years, she still likes it when I comfort her.

Meanwhile, grunts in their bunks pounded their salamis to a memory of the mortars' deathbeat drawing closer while drowning out whatever melodies once tricked them into sleep.

It's night when Jimi arrives via cassette. If you're a "head" you light up a Bong Son Bomber, let your imagination fly. Striding along a watchtower, Jimi cringes in the wind. Below, a grunt fallen in a firefight jumps bleeding to his feet. Watching closely, Jimi spots an amputated VC dick hanging, a talisman, from a string around the grunt's neck. The dick bounces up and down on the grunt's chest like a trampoline acrobat as the wounded buy spastically turns in circles, then again crumples to the ground. Chuckling to himself, Jimi thinks, *Crazy, crazy.* Suddenly, however, he feels depleted. Wanting only one thing now, to rest his senses, he finds the watchtower's quietest corner, sits on the floor, his back against the wall, then ties off, finds a vein & injects himself, knowing even soldiers of the heart, as opposed to soldiers on the ground, can step on magic tripwires & find a home that can't be reached otherwise.

COMMUNIQUÉ TO OUR CHEERERS AT HOME

Inside the rice kernel in the pod atop the stalk,
ungrasped futures wait.

Meanwhile, back home in open-air arenas crowds roar as guitars wail and
        the speakers' feedback sounds like minds going haywire..
Haight-Ashbury fades as a drunk stumbles out of the Venus Diner on 8th St.
        in New York City while in Indochina
a stoned grunt finds in the midst of a village field's silence
a monk tunneling downward through stony dirt
toward the Buddha's lap. In the end
it all comes down to this—
we're here, not back there, & wherever we go, & whatever we find, we keep
traipsing & the days
never end while the Buddha's lap
grows fatter after
every meal.

No one tells us. The wise just *know*—
we're the ones fucked, not you.

GETTING IT DONE

In the midst of a firefight, in epiphany's lonely corner when the time's right,
only Mama Morphine focuses on
the omens in the squashed centipede's belly
when Spec-4 Brown collapses to the ground.

Also, she's the one who deciphers his future in the blood-splatter patterns
where his left leg, from the knee down, explodes
into Kingdom Come.

That's when she casts a mellow spell on him, after which he blabbers—

Eensi meensi minsee Jeezus please.

Blades whipping up a gale, a chopper lands. In
a stupor, Brown stares dully to the side, then closes his eyes.
No hippie in a commune back home gets
this wasted. It's a special version of
elevated—

a deathzone shithole sundae of evaporating brainpower. Man, it makes you
        high! After that
your taste buds tingle.

Mama Morphine's done her job.

OUTLIVING THE DEAD

In blistering heat
the platoon marches. Bone-weary. Silent. Just when we think
we can't stand it anymore, Hartman's right boot
hits a tripwire, after which he receives
a free bodybag and an Ohio homecoming parade.

Don't kid yourself. It's not blood & guts
but the sacred which lures us on.
Look at how the napalm flame-wave, billowing forth from between
prophet Ezekiel's teeth
while Yankee Doodle cheers him on, leaves
a holy silence in its wake.

Awed, we stand
in unity. No single tab
of LSD reveals to us so well
the theatrics God has up his sleeve.

A VISIT WHILE IN BASE CAMP

Unable to think straight, he couldn't
 describe it right, although he tried. *It*
were the thigh wound started it
he said, then added, *And the fly larvae*
 that're in it now don't help either,
plus the artillery noise, it freaked me bad. He told me

all this yesterday. As he sat silently then, a line
of daylight cut across his bed like one side of a triangle
unlike any Pythagoras ever spied. This wasn't a world the kid recognized.
Nothing fit in place. But he
was stubborn, didn't stop
studying his location, peering around through drug-dazed eyes. Today

the drip
in his arm gives him what he needs: more strength, at least enough to get by.
Oh
here's Bobby, the kid grins just above
a whisper, pleased
to see me. No story
about the thigh wound today. That reality
has left his system like shit into the shitter. His new story's different. *Hey*
Bobby he asks

when they gonna fix my back concussion, I still
can't walk and I'm goin nuts and hafta
get outa here, you know?
Yeah I know, I answer, scrutinizing
him, 19 at most, a faker the brass calls him.
A faker maybe but one thing he doesn't fake well is sanity. Look at him.

The way
he holds his head up high right now trying to smile
but unsure why—
nothing will ever again hide
the unfeigned terror in his eyes.

You caught the fever, then your nerves went bad

for William Edgar John, 1937-1968

Under the parrot's wing, night makes no sound.
A stream, only a trickle, winds between trees
like a wish hunting a way out of Nam.
I follow it until I see faces that can't see me.
A dogbone lies in the dirt behind the house,
I'm stoned on the porch, a deviled egg in my mouth.
This is home, I think, unaware of where I am.

> *8 to 20 in the Walla Walla pen,*
> *you killed a man over a woman.*
> *Little Willie John, you did it now,*
> *you're really gone, a birdy in the prison.*

The bamboo thicket hides what it knows.
The water buffalo's unrevealing eyes frighten me. In
the LZ, dust whirls in the chopper's windstorm, each
dust grain a syllable in a language minutes old.
Schmidt's drawstring pouch with cut-off ears in it
is all I have for you—
an audience that won't care if you sing out of tune.

> *When you first sang at the Apollo*
> *wasn't a lady there didn't swoon.*
> *A promoter crowed, That guy's sound*
> *is like honey drippin' from the moon.*

Hey Willie, folks here worship ancestors
in corners in their huts, let's us do it too.
Let's carve an Eve from Brown's missing leg and construct a Nativity scene
from del Manzano's guts

and let's praise over there the evangelist
who's sanctifying everything nobody we know will ever get to touch.
Oh the Holy Ghost, loving disguises, is attired in camouflage tonight while
    last year when Motown burned It duded up like a pusher & sold
    folks bags of smoke for twenty bucks a piece.
Just what you need! the Holy Ghost announced, coaxing buyers toward
    paradise.

You began singin' gospel in Detroit,
you ended a dead bluesman in prison.
You sang with a heart all your own
while U.S. lies glared in bright neon.

ELISEO DEL MANZANO'S FINAL SONG

Day in, day out, I was tough as nails
until they dumped my guts in a pail.
Lifting Lady Morphine's dress
I found true boogaloo, was blessed.

Still, what I wanted then was to be returned
to El Fanguito, my barrio, as a living legend.
Instead, I found a grave near a fetid swamp.
No Taino songs then. No Lucita. No final romp.

O mamá, our family's holy one, lit up
by starfields, sipping blood from Jesus' cup.
I sinned by dying first. Now in the rain
you die alone, nursed by rotting plantains.

Meditation on the endlessness of it

A tropical French plantation
faraway. White sludge
from the gash in
a rubber tree trunk oozes
into a pail which evolves, somewhere
in America, into the palm
of a boy's hand as he lies
relieved & trembling
in bed on a sweaty August night.
That boy is me, years ago.
Now I'm here. Fighting
in Indochina for my life.

The dragontail butterfly's
weight, barely
detectable on the green
Vietnamese leaf, is capable
on certain days of breaking
men into pieces, then letting them
bleed out. So, not only
enemy fire takes our lives, but
also the undefined spying on us
from paddies, hootches, shadows &
the Tan Cang Bar's many eyes.

Everywhere, the unknown lurks,
breeding new logics that prevail.
Note how quickly
the repulsive settles in as normal—
only a few faces tattered by AK-47 fire are required
to find such scenes unworthy of a stare. And what

about Jesus, glowing in the stained glass window
above the altar back home? Kneeling
in prayer, elbows on a rock in Gethsemane—how quaint he seems,
stupidly
believing he's unique, that it's

his manifest destiny to redeem what remains
of our souls. How
outmoded! And yet
in spite of deriding him, here
I am, obediently in stride

as his general Uncle Sam guides me along
a road of defoliated credos
to the Promised Land.

Meat Puzzle

Smear your morning toast with del Manzano's sweet brainjelly, please.
Now peek between seen & unseen
to find a newborn truth. It'll be the one
in clean swaddling clothes
crying in the grass behind
County Park's outdoor stage from which
forked tongues speak
on Holidays.

At last the moment's arrived!
Be quick now, don't hesitate—
eat the placenta splattered near the newborn
on the ground. Next
lick the blood from any random face torn apart
by an M-16. Now you know
what it's like to excavate
what the mind's buried, that there's
no meaning that can explain
why you might be but aren't
alive behind the eyes.

Slow sex in a cramped room
with a bargirl from the Tang Cang
makes cats screech outside. Or is it
this that does it—how
one of us dragged a papasan
a month before to his death in a pretty
delta ville? Startled at that moment

by a white-throated kingfisher's red beak
as the bird flew in bright sunlight
across marshland, I felt uplifted. The beak's
still vivid now & so's the slow sex
& periodically the exploded dead—
bleeding jigsaw puzzles sold by vendors
with no eyes to buyers with no choice
in a marketplace run
by men named only in files marked *Classified.*

Last trek in country

Driving monsoon rain. Can barely see. By
mistake, we maneuver too close, slithering
on our bellies through mud. Above, the pilots
don't know. The bomb lands, the nearby
pagoda explodes. Shock waves shudder
through us like the Holy Ghost, making us
speak in tongues. My body shakes. Too
terrified to leave, I close
my eyes. Pretend to hide. Tell myself
No one can find me now.

Another day. A face
rots in swamp water, bits of it floating away
like tiny pieces of decayed bird feather.
That night, a few grunts scratch
crotch rashes as they suck reefer, after which
they listen to what the shadows say.
Still others, in a state of tense expectation, blank
their minds, intimidated by why
the poisonous pink oleander
whispers to them.

One day slogging across the boiling delta, something
within us rebels, leaving in its wake
a tiny craving to stomp out the flames sweeping
through trees into rice fields
where old mamasans, growing more spiritual
by the second, go up in smoke. As does
the craving, fragile as
a burnt baby's eyelid. Fortunately

some of us survive. Although
we leave behind
who we were before we arrived.

Anyway, no need to panic now. Home
from war for months, five of us remobilize
in Manhattan. Stoned insane, we go
on a recon mission, stowing away
on a ferry to an island in the city's
famous harbor where we stand,
posing for tourists' Polaroids
while holding the Statue of Liberty's hand.

Remembering January 11, 1967

4 a.m. After scissoring off what was possible
I razor-shaved
the beard stubble that remained, then
while rinsing my face
listened to the wind hissing past
Bianchi's Deli down the street.

What I dreamt earlier that night
is long gone now, as are
the cellars of condemned buildings filled
I imagined as a kid
with escaped jailbirds and spies lying
in wait for boys
with nowhere to go. Gone, too, is
the one-eyed monkey I saw in a carnie sideshow
in Queens when I was five
whose stare made me think
he could read my mind.

But back to that morning. Later
I boarded a bus with other guys
outside the local draft office in
the predawn cold for our trip
to Ft. Hamilton in Brooklyn.
In less than an hour, the morning's
final dark faded as the driver veered
onto a military entrance road
while behind us a tidal strait, the Narrows, reflected
the growing light. A few
minutes later, we stopped

in a parking lot where MPs studied us
as we disembarked, then entered
a building where all the hallways led
it was alleged
to the same culmination—
our maturation into men.

Meanwhile, far away, at
a paddy's edge, a baby rice shoot, fragile
as whatever binds the mind together, trembled
between a dead dog's splayed legs
trying to tell us something.
Not there yet, we couldn't hear it.

Only after months of training
did we arrive. In the un-
relenting sunlight in that burning land. Preparing
for sleep that night, we each
speculated privately about
who among us, having won
an unnamed game of chance, would tomorrow
or the next day be the first
to die, thereby
outfoxing the brass & going home, having found
the only AWOL you can count on.

HOMECOMING

A cab backfires. You scramble toward a nearby
hootch. A VC leaps out, holding
his AK47, bayonet pointed forward.
You shoot, he goes down, dropping not
a rifle but a hoe before he hits the ground.
That night before sleep, you replay
the moment in your mind. Repeatedly. No
two portrayals are the same. But that's

over now. It's rush hour, keep your head on straight.
Jampacked traffic inches west on 34th.
Worried, you walk in the same direction, engulfed
in a cacophony of horns, noisy mufflers, voices, sirens.
Distracted, you strain to stay
focused, every movement a prayer
to stay alive. As you eye each inch
of ground for tripwires, you swear
through clenched teeth
you won't get blown to bits before
you burn another Cong ville to the ground.

Before this, but even now

Like del Manzano at Tây Ninh, the wind
limps in blood-filled boots, flattening
tall grass. Not far off

the bamboo thicket's stillness swells
like the imagination on Demerol
back home. Wait. Once again

the sniper targets del Manzano, hits him
in the neck. Years later

the sniper shoots me too, striking
what I think I know but don't—your body's
feel. As I stroke your hip, it slopes

toward things just beyond my reach— every other
part of you, all unknown to me because

you are here in a future
I can't find. I'm still
back there, held in place

by Victor Charlie. It never ends.
Weapon fire sprays everywhere. Del Manzano
and Schmidt and Little Larry

go down

always
for the count

A MEMORY OF AARON'S RETURN

Light as the wasp wing in the porch corner,
the weight
of what will never be.

A rabbi visited, rang the bell.
From inside
Aaron saw thick eyebrows squashed
like two dirty rags
against the door window.
He didn't answer.
After a while, the man turned away.
A few days later, the rabbi came again.
Wasn't invited in then, either.

Time tells this story—
water sucks whatever it finds
from cracks in the nearby jetty's stilts;
an infant cries for its dead mother.

Back from war, Aaron avoids
telephones, government notices, the local synagogue.
A year later, he wakes
in the middle of the night.
as the child claws its cell's wooden bars
with uncut fingernails the size of owl beaks.

One day I arrive. To say hello.
The rice paddies are almost all burned, I say, standing
in the doorway.
Who are you? Aaron asks, refusing to let me in.
He's drunk, with an infant in his arms.

The wife's absence, still there, wider
than the bay on a winter evening.
Wind pounds the storm windows
day and night.

Working for the municipality, he plows
snow from roads.
An hour later, the plowed road:
snowed under again.

Only the Dark Makes Sense

Although I could walk straight, the way
the telephone poles leaned over
the garbage cans in search of scraps to eat
told me I'd drunk too much & so
shouldn't trust my judgment.
On top of that, Jamila, jittery
and shivering in a sweater too thin to protect
a mosquito,
gave me a look that had nothing
to do with love.
"So, soldier-boy, were you a good or bad kid in
that godforsaken jungle, eh?" she asked, then added,
"Well, my cousin told me *Está loco, hermanita* & that counts
for something, I guess." Which is when
we entered the 8th Ave. automat
where we located her friend Louis in a corner
eating eggs and home fries on a plate
smoother than the Plexiglas shields
behind which truth's alleged armies march,
gas-masked and bearing
clubs and guns.
 "You must be Jamila's cousin's friend from the army,"
he smiled, his thick
jetblack hair pulled back in a ponytail,
"Yeah, that's me," I returned his smile.
A few minutes later, while sipping our coffee, Jamila laughed
then produced a photo from her purse, saying
"This was taken when I was six."
A little girl in cowboy hat
pointed her pistol at an unseen enemy, who
she explained
was a gringo Jesus garbed like a sheriff who stood

near a plantain tree by a corral
outside the picture.
Later, after leaving, the three of us
spotted baggy human shadows huddled around flames leaping
from metal drums in an alley.
It was almost dawn
& I felt a headache coming on.
Shaking by then, I knew
daylight was dangerous
& only the dark made sense. So many
unlit spaces in which
to hide.

For all of us, there's something

It starts this way. Out of nowhere, a name
pops into your head. *Hartman.* The fellow
who got cut up real bad
by a tripwired explosive. It's all
so clear. How, with him squealing like a pig
in your arms, his blood soaks
through your shirt. That's
when you hear all the tugboats back home
in the East River sink. Yet
months later when your tour of duty's done
& you're back in the world again, the tugs
are still there, drifting aimlessly
like dead whales in the wrong waters, their
blubbery bodies covered
with large unfathomable wounds. How
they got there doesn't matter—
only their presence does. Soon
the tricks your mind plays on you
teach you everything you don't want to know
about how years of night-sweats
& screaming in your sleep
are only a fraction of what lies ahead.

I'M NO DOCTOR

for Steve from American Legion Post #1636, Brooklyn

Like you, I'm no doctor.
I barely know how to remove splinters
let alone insert steel pins
in the mind's cracked bones,
mine or yours or anybody else's.
What I do know, though, is how some philanthropist
should place a million buck reward on the head
of whatever creep forced you
to your knees, then made you pay a heavy price
when all you wanted was to stride forth
upright, no longer weighed down
by all that armor, those medals you earned in Nam
for being one of the nation's
more successful killers.
Now nothing helps. Not even a double dose
of meds stops you from sleepwalking down
your street in the dead of night until
by an accident of fate you can't explain
you awaken from your jaunt
trapped in a cramped space, gazing through
a lonely barred window, outside of which
an orderly you forgot was there
stands guard.

MEETING ELISEO DEL MANZANO'S COUSIN THE SECOND TIME

Two nights ago, she told me about
the last time she saw Eliseo, how
from the other side of a room
in a Harlem warehouse
El Oso, a guy with crooked nose, shouted to her
Hey Jamila!
as a defeated rooster, not dead yet
from the cockfight, bled
a hint of roses on
the floor.
After waving to him, she embraced
her cousin who was leaving
the following morning for the Nam.
Now, three years later, he's dead. But as I told her
later that night, already months before he died
he had a close call, his chest lacerated
from a fragmentation grenade's explosion.
I then added how weeks after the wounds healed, he
got sloshed one afternoon in the Tan Cang Bar, ripped open
his shirt &, laughing, told a crew of us
in a thick-tongued outburst
how the scars looked like ancient symbols carved
by his ancestors on Puerto Rican boulders. Then,
his mood quickly changing, he punched his breast
&, unnerving a bargirl
listening nearby, staggered
toward her, hollering
You betteth tell me what these goddamnth marks mean or elsth!
His body then went limp as he started
sobbing, then babbled to the woman he was sorry
as he reached out unsteadily
to hug her. She shoved him violently away.

As I told Jamila the story, she stared
straight ahead, then
when I was done
downed another shot of rum, grabbed
my hand & said
Don't take this wrong, but I'm getting the hell
out of here & I don't want you to come.

REVELATIOON'S WAY

War came easy to him. Not
the killing but sitting motionless
in a jungle LP at night. Focus
was his thing. Already
at 13, not moving
a muscle, a 12-gauge across his lap, he hunched in predawn dark
in a low sedge-covered boat, waiting
for ducks to give themselves away. It wasn't
the marksman in him who described this to us
years later, but the part of him that could identify
a duck's wingbeat
even before the sound wave arrived.

One day in Nam while waiting to find out
if back home wife Myra had given birth yet, he squatted
close to the ground to study
a red dragonfly flit from leaf to leaf. He was trying
he told us later
to define if their was a pattern
to how the dragonfly decided
which leaf to alight on next.

Rainy night. A moving van skidded
into a Ford & pinned it against a tree, killing Myra.
The baby, Rachel, was ok, babysat
by an aunt in Copiague. After
being called in by his Commander, Aaron
goes home on emergency leave

& few weeks later receives a hardship discharge,
the war behind him now.
Lucky bastard, Schmidt mutters days later
back in the Nam to Eliseo as they hunch
stoned in a ransacked hootch
adrift in delta mist.

When he first arrived home, whenever
the baby dozed Aaron imagined the sound Myra's eyelids made
when they closed the final time. It was
he claimed later
a noise like something in a Torah story
he remembered from when he was a kid—the faint whisper
of God's voice talking to the Prophet Elijah
in the quiet following a storm.
But God was gone now & Aaron didn't care,
so he pulled himself together, dug in
for the long haul, nothing
to live for, except
baby Rachel.
As she grew older, he sometimes believed
his worst days mentally
were his best as a dad—
that his withdrawals schooled her in how silence meant
not only words' absence, but the condition
from which they are born.

Less by choice than something fated, Rachel
emulated Aaron, learning the link between
his look—lips pulled back, teeth clenched—in response

to a bite of uncooked rhubarb
and the way he told the story about
the big duckfarms near Moriches. How
more than a decade earlier
their runoff leeched into the bay, killing a certain algae
and the oyster beds died out.
Never underestimate the unexpected, he told her more than once.

Soon enough she'd memorized the way
he navigated life to the tempo
of waves lapping and waves growing still, of
noise and silence. It was
revelation's way, the cadence
of tranquility & car wrecks,
of *before &* wars that tail your thoughts
into nightmares, from which
you strain to awaken
alive for another day.

WHEN IT DOESN'T COME TOGETHER EXCEPT IN NIGHTMARES

Bending over, Aaron's work buddy Chugger, un-
shaven, big gut flopping over belt, drags
the manhole cover—it makes
a loud grating sound—across
macadam, away
from the opening as I turn over
in my sleep & wake up, undershirt
soaked with sweat, head
aching from the cover's jarring noise. Getting
out of bed, I grope
to the bathroom. A single
gulp of water from the paper cup, then
back to sleep. Hours later
I wake again, drugged
in a hospital with Chugger standing
over me, blurting
They need you at work to fill
fuckin potholes, hurry up! I know
 he's drunk again, days
of stale booze on his breath, ever since
Aaron's return
from the Nam with a bag
of pumpkin seeds in his hand and now his little girl Rachel, arms
wrapped around his legs, whining
for daddy's attention.
Out of nowhere
my Uncle Bill appears in the doorway.
Better get outa bed and dress up
for church, he advises softly, then wipes
a toast crumb
from the corner of his mouth
with the back of his hand.

I fall asleep,
wake up once more,
it's dawn, no one's
in the house.
My underclothes still soaked, I don't
know what to do.
The goddamn roadwork won't ever end
I think, while outside
the July sunflowers loom, large enough to flog
  a panicked baby
senseless. Chugger, his beer belly
flabby but his upper body
strong, raises
the manhole cover above his head and shouts
I won't go quietly!
I WILL
fight back!
When was this? Or . . . did it
even happen yet?
My mind's a concentration camp—anything
that tries to sneak in or break out ends up
hanging by its skin
from barbed wire, dead.

WHEN DID I RETURN?

for Diana

I can't keep my eyes open
but can't sleep either.
Snowy February gusts rattle windows,
but somewhere else.
Other grunts sleep, fart, cough, scratch
their balls, wake up babbling.
I need sleep.
To create the mood, I carve your name
under my eyelid with a knife
so I can read it repeatedly, like counting sheep.
Already I'm drowsy.
Windblown snow pummels the windows.
I can't wait until morning, I'll get up and take the Chevy
for a ride through the white-out,
all the roads covered, not one building visible, only
me and the blizzard
on the move—
it's like the old days, I still have a knack for getting around!
Remember that one winter day in high school, me drunk
and you a budding hippie, how we
danced by ourselves in the freezing cold
in an abandoned gas station
once peopled by cool dudes filling their tanks
before taking joyrides
to wherever that place is
depicted in all the TV ads. Time
to refocus, though.
First thing in the morning now.
Must disassemble, clean, reassemble my M16.

We're headed in country today.
But. Where was . . . A few snags bewilder me. Out
of how many snowdrifts did I have to shovel myself
to leave home, and did I
arrive back in Nam before sarge noticed
I was gone?
And if so, why did what happened happen
outside the range
of what memory needs
to remember for the mind to resist
unraveling at the seams?

Jamila

She once told me how, late
one afternoon while visiting her father
in Puerto Rico near Jobos Bay's mangroves
where the mud flats flood in spring, she watched
a flamingo stand motionless in water, a vision
she proclaimed
of beauty freed
from human logic.

A year later, in an alley alongside
the Diamond Club in the Bronx, she concretized the phrase
A poem must look like this
by slicing her forearm with a knife.
Although I knew I should, I couldn't
look away.
How presciently the dark blood oozed into my life.

More is her only goal.
Disassembling totalities, she reveals
pieces, mysteries. The sea's undertow. How
the unripe *quenépa's* yellowish pulp ripens. Why
one-third of all island women
once were sterilized. The secret
of how to burrow with bare hands
in ordinary dirt to find meaning's roots.

Survival. For her, it means learning from
the nun at prayer. A type of holy fervor
disguised as cold deliberation. See
how she concentrates on each
of her location's details—like an iguana
studying a hornworm
it's about to snag between its teeth.

El Fanguito

for Elesio del Manzano, 1946-1968

Wrapped in a blanket stinking of fish, she gazes out
at what's disappeared: the toddler chewing
a breadcrust in the dust. You.

Tell your mother to stop looking, Elesio.
You're gone, and your brother Diego, well . . .

The heart died, the tidal marshes smell
and now the loan payment's due.
Tonight when the bomba drums thunder
even your nonexistence won't protect you.

Making tea, squatters boil shadows in a pot.
From somewhere else, the fried plantain's scent
arrives, an awakening
like the Virgin's nipple stiffening in the Christ child's mouth.

Oyeee! Let's dance tonight!
Moon lava drips through roof cracks, lighting
corners filled with the unseen's permutations
while beyond the slum's borders
the maggot plays guitar in the café of the dead tanager's gut! Listen
to it sing *mi querida hermanita*
to the nun's daughter screaming
at her junkie lover as he jabs the syringe in
his arm, killing
history's linearity and making the palm tree stand still in the windy night.
Ah, here in love's slum, God

is the fungus that grows in the petri dish
between the legs of the beaten hygienist pimped by a mafiosi disguised
        as freedom's Don Juan.

I'm here, but not you. Dressed
as silence's compañero, branches
tied to your helmet, you hide far away, a stag
in the underbrush, and wait.
Who would've thought it's deer season along the Mekong?
One shot and you fall. Antlers scrape dirt.

Listen how back home the bomba drums deafen!—the surly sea pounds
        rocks, the inchoate roars its meanings.
No tourist should visit the beach tonight. There, each mugger's a mystic
        who knows if he breaks open a skull he'll find an angel to fondle.
(*May I*, he'll beseech his prey, *remove your wings?*
May I whip your flesh until it bleeds with a knowledge of the unforeseen?)

And so. And then.
Your cousin Jamila's Uncle Jimmy once grew cucumbers and tomatoes
not far off. Now
a petrochemical factory's there, disgorging smoke
blacker than a Taino's nostril hairs.

Rooster with a pecked-out eye,
blood on the abandoned warehouse floor,
cops track down the cockfight,
everybody stampedes out the door.
Tan dónde están usted, Elesio, heh?
In the end, our sobs can't pay the rent.

The stench of puked flounder on your mother's blanket. The stomach
cancer did it
and too many other things to count.

GRILLED BURGERS, MEMORIAL DAY,
FOUR YEARS AFTER RETURNING TO "THE WORLD"

I remember looking
at it. Where
you'd placed it in the backyard grass

next to your lawnchair—the
artificial leg. Later
from another position
I studied its absence, a shaft of empty air

where your real leg once angled
downward from just above the knee
to the ground. But that wasn't all
that had disappeared. There was . . . Forget it. We don't need

another old story. Anyway, the sunlight
was too bright
that afternoon & I felt lightheaded. For a moment
I was unsure where we were. Another beer
followed by a shot of Jack
didn't fix my head. All I know is
all at once we were stumbling forward, humping
the boonies, then later we released
magazines of rifle fire from a treeline, choppers
overhead, people in pajamas darting through
elephant grass near a village, all this
while daffodils fluttered
in the breeze by
a boulder ten yards behind
where you sat that holiday while you told Ellie, still

your wife at the time, *For all the shit*
we've been through, I still hold down a steady job
and do . . .
Which is when she cut you off, mocking
your tone as she finished your sentence—
and do . . . my bit to drink and dope away our cash. Every detail

of that day still exists. I remember
it all. Even how
later, still
drinking, I blurted jokingly, after
glancing at the little garden
by the boulder—
                                   Those flowers, yeah
they're nice alright but I can't help thinking if
your thick head hadn't forgot
your friggin leg back in the Nam, they'd
be prettier. To which Ellie

always listening
snapped

You two just can't stop, can you! She
was right, I guess, although
you angrily disagreed, scooping up

your fake leg from the grass, then heaving it

at the cellar door, breaking
its window as you yelled

I don't WANT to stop! Which is when
Ellie, body clenched, commented
icily —

I know what's required,
I'm gonna light up the coals
then grill you boys some burgers
after which you can choke to death,
I don't care.

The few

Trinh Van Loi, our translator, was religious, more monk than grunt. He got on my nerves sometimes like when—I'd known him for months by then—he quoted the Buddha to me during a conversation we had while I smoked a cigarette outside an abandoned hootch.

Repeating lines from an old text, he told me, "Just as there's no place to hang paintings in the sky, so when you think clearly illusion has no space in which to live."

That and a cup of coffee won't save my ass from booby-traps, I figured.

"You understand?" he wanted to know.

"Understand?" I asked, perplexed. "Understand what?"

"Understand that 'thinking clearly' means to go beyond the way we usually think. When we find the end of the old way, when we overcome belief and discover 'the nothing,' that is when we truly begin to live."

"The nothing! I already found that!" I answered sarcastically. "Where you been? There are fuckin' corpses everywhere. They're the nothing. But they're still goddamn real."

"Sorry," he replied grudgingly, then continued, "I should not have said anything, I'm tired. But I thought you might get it. I wanted—"

Now I was really pissed. "Shut your fucking foodhole!" I cut him off. Who the hell are you to tell me what I know and don't know?"

"No one," he answered. "No one finds truth for anyone else. You're right."

Exhausted from talking, I teased him by pointing my M16 at his head. "Maybe I should just shoot you," I joked, "and rearrange your brain."

"Can the dead kill the living?" he snapped pompously. He apparently believed being a smart-ass would show me he wasn't going to let me push him around.

"I was just fucking kidding," I replied. I felt like slamming him in the face with my weapon. In my head I saw him fall to the ground after I hit him. But I held back.

But that wasn't the worst of it. After a brief return to base camp, our unit was back in country again. Days passed. Fields became more densely overgrown and paths more tangled and what the locals said became more nonsensical whether translated or not. Everything was out of whack. Like the time a pagoda gong's sound seemed to emanate from inside a small bowl of fish sauce on the floor of an abandoned hootch we explored during a search-and-destroy caper. Finally, we trudged away, heading as always further from home while at the back of our minds there was—what? Everything was askew. Jungle rot ate mole holes between our toes. Descriptions of what was going on were aborted in our brains by a cocktail of insanity, anxiety and longing. Is someone singing? And if . . . which is only —

Cong tunnel under here?
Cong tunnel under there?
Sniper hide where?
Red-whiskered bulbul
sings everywhere.

Each day the platoon's fate became more entwined with the tempos of things unseen. A Charlie finger scratched a mosquito bite. A thought faded as a VC fell asleep near a delta stream.

Something was out there. But where?

We walked and walked. The stones under our feet were scrambled prophecies we couldn't read.

Everywhere we went, waterbuffalo eyes perched like scavenger crows in our mind's trees. At night the mist, sliding over stones and fence posts, woke us up.

More alive than ever before, many of us died. Those who didn't carried those who did on our backs for the rest of our lives. Once back home, we pulled up manhole covers, then climbed down into the sewers below, beyond the government's reach. Although we didn't know what to do next, we kept marching out of habit. Each morning when we awoke after a night asleep, we found ourselves still marching, indeed had marched while we slept, searching, always searching for a place to tell our tale. Although we didn't know exactly what our tale was, we were certain we'd recall it by the time someone asked us to hear it, but nobody did.

New Orleans psalm

Last night a sick bird, shrieking
on the hotel roof, woke me up.
Now I sit outside warmed by the sun
under a balcony on which
a potted lily blooms.
I look at passers-by
while Johnny D., the guitarist on the corner
plays his morning hello, simultaneously plucking strings and
　　　　thumping wood.
So many things have happened here.
Martha, who lives behind e grocer's, told me,
First I painted an old cigar box yellow, then afterwards
because I had the urge
I covered it with orange animals.
Later, I walked down an alley, swung open
the gate at the end, wandered
a few blocks, then circled back, not to the hotel
but to the first time I saw
one of my mother's bloody pads in the toilet, thinking
at the time how
Jesus the punisher must have hacked off her penis for being bad.
A child, I spoke as a child, but when. . . As I grew up, sky
was the dividing line between low and high,
the gigantic's two sides—
time and whatever time isn't.
Live long enough and soon the evening shadows become
the ashes we smear on our bread before we gorge on it
as the unknown appears where
no one knew it could—this time
where a water moccasin glides into view inside a tear
falling from a child's eye.
I sometimes think pain is nothing but

pleasure seen incorrectly, Leon "Monsieur" LaCount, a Vietnam vet
 and Buddhist masseuse meditates out loud to me
over a late-night whiskey in a bar.
Later, I sit in the same chair in which I sat this morning.
Gone now, Johnny D's
somewhere in the night, singing praises to the Lord
while the rotting magnolias' scent reminds me
of beauty more than the magnolias did
when they were alive.

The signs were there

for Rachel

When you were little, what he sensed
in silence you translated
into sounds.
By softly beating your lips, you made the noise
off a darning-needle's
flapping wings.
To evoke falling asleep, you tamed
your breath, teaching it to scrape
like wind through water reeds
in dying light. To tell
grief's story, you created a raspy humming, one
 with a tune that came
and went and sometimes, but not often, produced
a word, a distorted ah or oh
that slowly disappeared again into your husky hum
like a clam burrowing in mud.
When in your teens you started mixing your sounds
with actual phrases, everybody knew
who you were—a social tease with a trick
or two up your sleeve, singing
"You Are My Sunshine"
as if it were an invite to the cops
to identify the crime on your mind
before you committed it. After that
it was no surprise when you
went pro as a singer. I still remember
the Brooklyn club where you started, how
the bass player produced a sound
as elegiac as the train to Rockaway Blvd. But it was you, new
to the scene, who

startled the crowd, turning your first song,
an old ballad, into
a gutsy convulsion, a spasm
toward something more than tradition allowed.
Later, whether the horn led you or you led it
didn't matter anymore. The quintet *swung*, a layering
of cross-fertilizations, each member
depending on the others
like grunts in cane grass under fire. Fitting in, you
improvised on the fly—
broke the storyline, scatted away from the words
or slipped into mellow or did down and dirty when
that's where the music had to go, anything to get to the bottom
of the beat, the utterness, of things.

"WHERE HAVE ALL THE SOLDIERS GONE?"

for Brown, not "all," but one

A one-room walkup no bigger than
a broom closet. More bunker
than a home. Dug in for the night,
your head stutters with weapons fire.
That was a year or two after
your second divorce.

When long before that, Lenny, your favorite
comic, got busted for
obscenity further north in a cafe on Bleeker St., you
were on the upswing. Getting drafted
was your chance. A door
swung open, you swaggered through. You figured
a War Hero was what the sweeties fancied
so that's what you'd be.

Didn't happen.
More than two decades later & there you were—two
divorces, kids & grandkids gone.
Climbing up four flights with a hightech leg
didn't turn the trek
to bourbon heaven more appealing.
Too much was missing. No pool table
in the den—in fact, there was no den. And the used Corvette
you planned to rebuild by hand sat on cinder blocks
in a driveway in an empty lot
miles from the walkup where you almost
died, a heart attack, five years ago today.

You visited me a few months after that. One afternoon
following a few hours of placing meager bets
on the horses at Belmont, we strolled
the mudflats along
Little Neck Bay. A foul odor oozed
from the ground and you started gagging. Before
I knew it, you were throwing up, your body
violently seizing as if disgorging
your whole friggin life.

By then, you'd already, unknown to me, said goodbye
to the old you as you searched for where
the bible's reborn serpent slithered happily in the shadows
while offbeat Saints learned to feed
like hyenas, ripping pieces of nutritious meat
from what was left of wisdom's corpse.
Sober after that, you worked days, attended
school at night & turned your words
into bayonets, hooting each time
you gouged holes in officialdom's
obese body of lies.

9/11 . . . Kingdom Come Arrives

A dead Albanian's ghost speaks to us from Macedonia

June 8, 2001, three months before 9/11

When first the stones crashed through the window
and the cake shop burned, the town of Bitola
was a goner. Everything
including the imagination
was under siege. Mobs
coursed through the streets, not
for love but obsessed
with setting mosque carpets on fire
and breaking Muslim gravestones into rock heaps
while further west Christians threw nets
like a comforting nostalgia into the Adriatic Sea
or mined copper in mountains
they declared were theirs.
Trembling, I remember nights so dark both mountain peaks
& water seemed afloat in a sky
more impenetrable than the abyss in a bigot's heart.
Yes, living here wasn't easy, except
for this—what I recall
of my wife's belly's curve, that gentle slope
toward all existence, and her mind
a falcon gliding wherever required for nourishment.
Even when rioters killed me because I quoted the Prophet's verses,
it was my wife's memory, nothing else, that reminded me of al-Lah, our Lord.
What the murders of so many of us
prefigures, I can't foretell, although I know
such chaos can occur anywhere.
So, if you receive this communiqué, tread carefully. Beware
your moral creeds don't propagate
the very hatred you claim to hate.

Moments: dusk to night

Sept. 11-13, 2001

Silence's birth: a dog
drools in the grass.

Later.
No, she tells the man,
I won't do it.

Trees, the tops of which
touch clouds. The dog's
gone. Through
the bushes behind the statue
of the war-dead in the park. Down
the unseen slope to the river.
Listen. Either wind
or water moves. This
should be remembered. Written down.

Why? he asks.
What? she answers, forgetting
her earlier words.

This is what's important—how,
from a playground we can't see, the girls'
jump-rope rhymes travel to us

through the cedars. Although we hear
only the rhythm, but not the words, this is
for the moment
enough for us.

Leave me be! she yells, yanking
an arm free from the man's grip. When
she goes, he walks the other way.

This is when night arrives, drifting toward
Mr. Red sitting on his porch
on 21st. And also arriving here
in the park, as the dog
returns, a thought
shitting in grass.

But what about, earlier,
the steel beam, how it
knocked sense into someone's head
as the tall building fell
into whose lover's arms?—

Knocked sense? Don't be surprised. Be forewarned.

The changes are incessant. Nothing's too small.
The racoon's paw prints years ago still befuddle us.
They stopped ten feet before the brick wall, yet
it somehow reached the open second floor window, entered, found
the crib and scratched the girl's leg.
I told you don't think about those things anymore!

her mother wrote years later in a note
to her daughter.
Leave me the hell alone! she scribbled in reply.

Tonight will be a night no one forgets.
After all, our memory of the leaves
on Mr. Bailey's peach tree 25 years ago
remains with us, as does
our vision of Sheila, the 13-year-old black girl
he shot in the back.
And what about two months ago? How
only blocks from here, Abdullah Alameri
who drove the Jack & Jill Ice Cream truck
was shot dead in the front seat.

And now?
Tapioca . . . pudding, it's . . . still my favorite, Pauley
answers his seated mom distractedly while leaning against
the living room wall, as he studies how
on TV the plane hits the building
like a flying bulldozer.

Later, when someone rings the front bell, he hurries
to the door, then leaves.

The night streets. They beckon us. See
how holy they are. Unprofane. *Ours.*

In the tree's shadow behind
the Watter's house, a swing

and broken rake. Is this
where the worm crawls through the dead robin's belly, climbs
upward through its throat, pries open the beak, then leaps out
& becomes the end
of what is known?

Years ago, on call, Dr. Rab arrived
with his syringe.
He's retired now. No longer calm,
I see
more sharply than back then.

Someone's been here. Look: footprints in the grass . . . down Monkey
        Hill. I go too.

At last. There's Mickey. And my two favorite lovebirds.
After a round of hellos, Mickey and I discuss the river's ideograms on
        the rocks
while Imani laughs when Leon, brushing
away mosquitoes with his hand, says
See how I did it? Sometimes
I disperse Allah's tiny parables just to let Him know I can.

Tomorrow the children will be tested
and so will the mums.
Some will survive.
Others won't.
How long will the coming wars last? That will determine everything.

Beyond the sentimental

Unlike the dead, I get to grieve the dead. Here is
a pig in a barnyard
in a children's book. Here
is the department store into which I traipse
through the revolving door and then emerge
again. Here is Amos
grouting tile in Mr. Herbert's tub. Each moment's
so full of here it's voluptuous,
with a luscious belly button and breath-
taking toes. This is what I get to know, which
the dead don't. Consequently, I don't grieve for them by wishing
it was me not them, but by being glad
I'm alive. If I were dead
who would remember what they can't?
The living's job is to create
a pedestal upon which to place
a bust of the uncertain, its large nostrils
quivering like a race horse's.
The only way to grieve
is to feed our babies ashes
while talking with the mullah and the abbess
about the complexities of *is*—
that dance of known and unknown, as pilots
explode in midair
and smoke rises everywhere.
Someone alive today
is better than someone dead. Ask the plains shaman
how to grieve the wild petunia
growing from a calculus of skulls. Stand solemnly
by the hearse with the state's poets if you want
to weep the tears of weepers
who love to weep. Real grief's

beyond the eyelash imitating
an eyelash in a poem. It requires
learning the crustacean's epics, the Kaaba's
black stone's silence, why Abu-Jamal
writes from death row but you don't, and other things
it's good for us
to figure out.

WRITTEN FOR SOMEONE TODAY

I would split a grain of salt
in half with a guillotine
if you needed only half. I would
be the bee, legs weighed down with pollen
as I trudged, barely able to navigate,
toward the petal's edge, where that wrinkle
at the corner of your mouth
seduces me as you stoop to look
at this flower. I would be
the silence's flamboyance, the way
it dresses in a gypsy shirt, half
unbuttoned, chest hair spilling out. If it were possible, I would even
skin myself and stretch
the resulting lace of flesh across those who lie
in ashes where the towers fell
so you wouldn't have to see them.
I would, but won't. Look. Everything
we think we know
should collapse like that.

A DAZED FATHER RELATES HIS DREAM

In it, I break open
a child's breast bone, reach
in and pull out
a fish from Lake Ronkonkoma
a long time ago.
"Very good," my weeping mother says while standing
next to me, "you did that nice."
After I throw the fish down, it flops
futilely around on a shore where nothing remains
but innuendoes, as ashes blow
in my eyes, making me rub them
until they throb.
Awakened by this, I shake my wife
by the shoulders, pleading "Help!"
But she won't cooperate, insisting
"You're still asleep, you just think you're not."
At that very moment our son calls from the other room
"It's nice visiting with you both again."
At first I feel delighted to hear his voice but then
remember he isn't home—he flew overseas
months ago for a tour of duty
in Kabul, then
was killed in Kandahar weeks later. The moment
I realize this I wake up again, bellowing at him
"Leave us alone you're dead!"
Once more my shouting rouses my wife who blurts
"You're definitely awake this time
and know what's going on."
Since then, rain threatens every day
yet we haven't seen a drop.

The only thing to do is wait,
but for what? is the question.
Each week the authorities promise
our son's body will be flown home soon
but no bodybag shows up for us
at the air force base.

Beyond sanctuary

Wet a.m. light coagulates on the maple branch,
dries, flakes and blows away.

You drive down a street
while somewhere else
another man's sperm dries
on your wife's thigh. As
the day wears on,
the jism disappears.

In the rocky place where desire ends, north
of a Kabul we don't understand,
a child is killed
by U.S. fire.
Upon a toenail's rubble
a new village will be built.

Something dries
on our hands then
flakes away, as do
the hands.

WHILE LISTENING TO SUN RA, THE SPIRIT MOMENTARILY STIRS

for Mary Stricker

Some in groups, others alone, all heading in their own
willful directions, the piano notes, like
pedestrians on the corner of 4th
and Market
on a sweltering day, zigzag

ahead in spite
of the heat. Sometimes they take
a few steps back
in order to re-

formulate ahead's meaning, thereby
adding to it something most
so-called progress forward doesn't have: an *attitude.* One

that revels in how the necks's
cut open to get at
a clogged carotid artery or how

a heart's accessed by cracking
the chestbone with an oscillating saw—all

traumas like these ruin what we know
about stability, yet also display how
disharmony, regardless of
the odds against it, is
a signpost along the way to finding

the melodious where
(most officials agree)
it can't exist

yet does. It's right there, for instance, where

Catherine St. deadends at 8th
and goatherds, glancing around
curiously, wander
down from the Pamir mountains

in Afghanistan straight into Philly
while kids in the park across from your house stop playing

and gaze at them
as in the background

—I hear it through my headphones now!—

the piano man
Sun Ra shows decades ago
how by including notes
known not to exist, the known disappears
replaced by a music

more multilayered, more
upward-downward, more
a method of experiencing the real
than was thought
viable before

Death prayer anniversary coda

first anniversary, 9/11

It's funny what you remember.
He was an old Italian whose larynx was removed
because of cancer and so spoke
through a mechanical voice box. That was back
in 1982 when he told me

in his robotic voice *They'll blow up*
some day, meaning, not
the Twin Towers, but
the apartments on Thompson St. where
he swore he smelled gas leaking
earlier that morning. It made him nervous

he confided
because of Bergheim's, the building super's, story
years before.
In it, a girl, looking up

into nonexistent water, inhaled
in another country
a surprise from the shower nozzle: the Jews'
collective destiny. But that's not
it. I've strayed. The nozzle isn't why

we mourn today. It's
because of the birds
screaming in the tulip poplars—
the amnesia in their eyes,
their misleading wings. It makes

us think. How at the edge of what we thought
we knew, leg hair
and so much else burned, part of the rubble
of fallen buildings
a day after the Broncos overwhelmed
the Giants by 11.

And so we mourn, our grief
now more tactical, an organizing principle .
In a village
in Uruzgan, drums boom in a mountain courtyard, women
sing, dancers whirl and swirl.
The chickpeas taste good. As do the olives.
But when
the bomb hits, the wedding reception ends, 54 guests
already dead.
From the roof, a panicked mother
drops her infant to the ground.
The strike was a mistake, the Pentagon announces later.

The days pass wearily. But in order. More comical
than decades ago, the TV ads
amuse us more than the shows.
Each evening is a lullaby.

But not the late afternoons. When the birds, screaming, gather
in the tulip poplars.
No matter what they don't know or remember, they understand
how to shatter silence and be heard.

Kingdom Come's Arrived

In memory of Balbir Singh Sodhi (1949-2001)
on the anniversary of his death, fours days after 9/11

1
Rowhouses, windows boarded up. Two closed auto plants. Another
          post-industrial futuristic city.
This one, though, is mine. We all
live somewhere.

Wherever you buy your black tar baggie
or Starbucks latte. Whatever day or year. No one
can avoid the codes. You either
break them or don't. One way
or another, they'll either boost or ruin you.
Make a wrong move,
your optic nerves burn out.

This is it. Home. The place
from which the soul branches out, sucked
into its own unique
gyre of years. First, there

& then here. I remember . . . Oh yeah. A visit. 1965. A cloud
of swarming mosquitoes on the Salt River's bank, a few miles
from where, thirty-six years later,
Balbir would be murdered. But not knowing

that at the time, I headed
southeast of the river & southeast of Mesa too, then
further still toward Mexico through Tombstone. But. No

youthful wandering today. It's

Sept. 15 again. Another year down the road
from Balbir's death. I remember a TV repeat
from a few days ago. In it, planes

crashed into towers, asbestos
dust & people floated
in air. Did the Chargers'
trouncing of the Redskins two days earlier prefigure
the ostentatious marvels that soon came? A week after
the buildings fell, anthrax-laced letters
arrive in newsrooms, showing us
we believed
how right our moral matrix is—no need
to analyze waking up, you just *wake up*. Being attacked's the same. No
hesitation, go
into action mode: *Onward Christian soldiers, onward as to.* Four
days later a door swings open. Frank
Roque rushes from

the Wild Hare Bar, climbs into truck, peels out enraged
and soon, parked again & looking out
the window, pulls his .380 handgun's trigger
five times & Balbir Sodhi Singh goes down for the count, a Sikh killed for
            what he wasn't. Muslim.
Oh, c'mon, it's an honest mistake. A turban's kinda like a kufi, everybody knows
            that, yesiree!

And so. Foes
kill three thousand of us & now payback's begun. We will. Yes
will. Kill them. Tens
of thousands of them, even if we can't identify who *them* is. Nonetheless. No
letup. 24/7 focus

required. Even the number
of petals on the chrysanthemums in an apartment's window boxes
might prove later to hold clues
about a household's covert chants to their deity. So much
hidden in the moment. Giant
industrial blenders chop, then puree
middle-eastern bodies into
protein smoothies which keep grunts' energy high.

2
Balbir went down. As in crumpled
to the ground. The sky
weighed so much
it flattened him. It was

a resolute assassination, although pulled off
by a shooter confused
about whom to pop. A Muslim
who's not a Muslim, what's that? Anyway
the first "enemy" slain
post-9/11 didn't know
where Medina or al-Zulfi in Saudi Arabia were or any of
Mohammed's bones, either. It was
Punjabi dirt from India between his toes, even when
he crouched for a minute's relaxation
in Mesa shade behind his Chevron station. But now, *ssshh,*
the funeral's about to begin.

The mourners gather. Watch how the cremation fire
migrates through the body, a mind traveling through a sieve.
Note the ceremonial dagger's ideal placement. Listen
to the night prayer intoned. Now shift your gaze
to the side. Observe
the stately government official, standing

rigid & alone. Or is it
the Empire itself, looking on, tears streaming, an
industrial cutting fluid, down
its cheeks, eating trenches
in its enigmatic face?
Beware, though, of what happens next. Frank Roque

fired his first shot in an instant. But its impact
reverberates even now, sounding
different day to day, as it will
year to year, always demanding
to be heard. So what do we hear? Is it

Col. Carson & his troops galloping through
an Arizona canyon, thieving
the indigenous' sheep, slaying people, razing peach orchards & laying
        down the law by lighting
cornfields on fire? Later
a lone Diné on flute improvises songs only desert-lovers hear. But what's
that other noise? Is it

the sound elsewhere of a puma as it slouches from one thought to another,
prowling
the narrow ledge between this and that, teaching us
cognition's power? Or is it

the Stenson Boys
playing banjos and thumping tubs up north
behind the Mt. Zion Grange? Or is it the hopeful echo

in people's minds
of Henry Ford slapping
the Grand Wizard's white-gowned back? Or possibly
it's all these noises combined, a din, a cry it's up to us to define.

3

In the end
the joke's on us, buried as we are
under memories we ourselves interred. Here
in this diaspora of our own making, we leave
only this behind—
a long-lost memory of deaths we declined ages ago
to admit were real, yet now gaze

at their faces. Inescapable. Right here. Listen to the voices.

> *He winced at the bite of the dogs the police used to chase him down. Then*
> *a gunshot rang out. Soon*
> *another. And . . . again.*
> *LA, New York, Birmingham, Ogden, Cleveland.*

Or this one.

> *Some called it a shithole, but it was punk's holy grail.*
> *There, one night a lead singer, held aloft, bodysurfed across*
> *the moshpit throng—his arms twitched & legs flailed*
> *to the beat of democracy's demented song, its lyrics drawn*
> *from a once living language now lynched & buried*
> *in an unknown location on the Washington mall.*

Each voice, a fading resonance. A match's frail wisp of smoke.
In the distance, old identities quiver
like the heat haze into which they disappear.
Another story evaporates, a new one
is born.

> *A nameless laborer, I broke rock for the open road.*
> *Later, I was a carter for a fire brigade*
> *until one day, fighting a boarding house's flames, a witness noted of my demise*
> *"Tumbling walls buried him in their debris."*

Look westward, sister, brother. Diagram all that's gone. Memorize how
      barren land stretches

to the horizon in every direction.
Big Daddy Country reduced . . . to dead nation.
Many times is how all this began.
One was Balbir's assassination.

There's always an afterwards

One vet gapes for days
at a jigsaw puzzle with lost pieces. Another
inches a walker down
a corridor, a hand grenade's pull-ring
clenched between his teeth. On a different ward
 an old chestwound smokes a cigarillo
in the outhouse behind its boyhood home
in a morphine dream in a triage tent
in a time warp too convoluted to unravel. Then

over there, where a returning hero
has bolted himself
inside a hospital bathroom, an army nurse yells
through the door☒
I know you're screwing around with your dick in there!
A culture unto itself, vet life

lurks everywhere. The homeless ones, gaunt
soothsayers ignored by their countrymen, emerge
from alleys, leaving behind, swaddled
in used candy wrappers, parables about
old gradations lost in Mosul firefights. Now, while one vet
departs from an alley, another
remains behind, seated knees to chest against
a dumpster, decoding
unknown addresses on crumpled envelopes. Simultaneously

vets whose nightmares already have left grease stains
on VA psych ward walls
huddle behind Lily's Jamaican Eatery, eying
the feral cat's untamed grace, its body's
sinewy patrol of this place of foregone extinctions.

Later, Brown, one-legged since Nam, shows me the letter
he once wrote his ex-wife about
the syringe's gift of revelation: how
mellow floats you to where the barn swallows are, after which, holding
your hand, something undefined bestows
its friendship on you & you know you're almost home. It's close

to midnight now & the moon
O the moon, the lovers' moon
is out!
How many of those we know tailed truth's ghost
into discernment's imbroglios—the ins
& outs, the ups & downs—then leapt
with their necks in a noose
from the moon?

MORE THAN ANOTHER NIGHT

In the fireplace, a fire.
The draft sucks smoke
upwards, ashes

fall through the grate—mindlfakes
floating between
whatever bars hold them in.

In the distance bombs whistle
once again through air, explosions
everywhere—wild lilies metastasize

in the body of the world.
In spite of the noise, I can hear
on the window's other side

the sound of snowflakes landing
on the ground. Earlier, unable
to reach my old Army buddy Aaron

by phone, I dialed Rachel,
his daughter. After answering, she
instantly broke the news—

I'm sorry. Papa died
five months ago. I couldn't
track you down.

DRUNK & DISORDERLY, SAYING GOODNIGHT TO GOD FROM THE GREENE ST. JAIL

Place your cock in your mouth, Holy Father. Suck
yourself to sleep while praying
for love in your own embrace. Forget the schizoids,

prophets and war-wounded, all of whom , like dogs,
piss on fire hydrants after lining up for hours
to receive a free lobotomy from clinics recommended

by the CDC. Disregard, too, your own mind, that space
in which Centaurus 99's quantum physics
rumbas on a dance floor you can't see. Have you

spurt your manjuice into your throat yet, then gulped it
down like sleep, while night rinsed
the iris stamens outside your palace gates?

Don't worry. If you panic in the dark, calm yourself
by contemplating uranium's half life
or the Dali Lama's popularity. But stay away

from Brooklyn where a plunger handle, shoved up
Louima's ass, soon became
a conductor's baton directing background music

for bombing Kosovo & Mosul as the moon's fuse blew
and more than the lights went out. Stop
whining, God. Close your eyes. Goodnight.

The locusts' vocabularies
—Iraq

I SEE IT

Rain pounds the street while the wind blows
the plastic lid off
the trash can as water splatters down
from the blocked gutter
above the kitchen window. On the TV
on the counter, a journalist speaks, on-site, face
to camera. Behind him
fleeing crowds swarm toward the desert south
of Najaf. Some say a newcomer
will soon arrive, his eyes
burning darkly, a hornet's black markings.
Trudging forward, he will guarantee, they say, a better life
even to the viper while handing out
sodas and candy bars to anyone who begs. Here
rain and there smoke rising from buildings
burning along night streets. Down
an alley where the stewed chickpeas' smell
thickens, thoughts
explode in people's skulls and bits
of bone fly like shrapnel everywhere.
Looking out
the window again, I gaze at closer things, how
rain batters car hoods while
Mrs. Dalia across the street on her front porch
unties her white hair, then shakes
her head, hair brushing
frail shoulders
more gently than one would think
possible now.

Uday al-Bakhir talks spontaneously in Tompkins Square Park

Forget about the hatred here. Mosque walls
spraypainted with insults. The guy
killed in Mesa. The convoluted logics that,
feeding only on dust, ashes & hysteria, nonetheless grow
from the towers' rubble. Instead

of these things, let's talk about *there*, that other place, Iraq, how

eventually the moonlight fades, replaced
by daylight, and so
it's morning again, although
the mind these days can't specify

exactly when night gives way
to light, or if the cupola, a different
blue than the sky's, is
a better blue or why
dogs now bark before, during
& after the muezzin's call
to prayer. This beckoning
rouses feelings no outsider
can understand, just as
when the wind blows, flinging sandgrains
at the camel's head, only those

of us born there know what being there now is like and how
it feels to realize
Iraqi deaths will be televised between two ads—one telling

your yellow ribbon wearers all they need to know
about the electric drill they want for Christmas
and the other guaranteeing that any sandwich meat with mustard or
      mayonnaise
on Sarah Lee whole wheat is ideal to eat
while downing a cold beer. But me

all I want is something from
back home—*basbousa,* the taste, the ground almonds, the syrup.
So much to recall. My mother once explained
to me how vaginas bleed and have needs
outside of what men say and do. Maybe to you this sounds
unrelated. However, if I change only a few words
in that statement I possess the perfect revelation for you Americans—

Iraqis bleed and have needs outside of what you fucking people say and do!

INTERSECTING ANGLES

When her husband's joke made her sob, she knocked
her gin fizz off the table
onto the carpet, attracting
other guests' attention. What,
Tom Brokaw wanted to know
behind her on the TV,
would the next move be? The camera panned
across desert sand while she screamed
at her Mr., *You keep changing the reasons*
you hate me! I can't stand it! On
her hands and knees now, she tried
to wipe up the spilled drink
with her handkerchief. Soldiers in a jeep
drove above her head toward a place she'd never visit. Her husband
ignoring her
pointed at the news anchor and remarked to Glen, his friend
It's impossible to tell what'll happen next.
People milled around, eyeing each other
uneasily. Soon
her husband's hand was under
her armpit as they walked out the door. After that
was a blur. Hours later she awakened
groggily as rainy daylight rinsed
her Bridgeport home's windows on a street
which skirted, like an idea
with little weight, past
whatever hope of meaning once existed. Something
escaped her, then. *But what?* she wondered, sitting
on the sofa where she'd slept.
Which was when she recalled what she glimpsed
a few days ago on TV. Soldiers
huddled on the ground, their eyes closed

in a violent sandstorm which blew
beyond them toward
questions with no answers. Meanwhile
to the north, Jonah, the old prophet
still railed against
Nineveh, bellowing how
if the city didn't surrender to God He would destroy it, setting
the temples on fire, black smoke
swirling everywhere. *What*
a day, she thought, still perched
on the sofa
as the morning rain, growing
more torrential, carried away
the names of continents and memories of movies
in which a poor kid turns to a life of crime
to buy his mom fur coats & a house.
What's that? the hungover woman suddenly grilled herself. A repeated
sound. Up stairs. *Thump, thump, thump.* Her husband
pacing back & forth. Then, silence. *But why?* she wondered, closing
her eyes. The soldiers, still
there, were only boys.
The sandstorm continued forever,
she flinched from every sting.

To Yasin Taha Hafiz

after crossing the border from Kuwait into Iraq

Like you, I spotted her. She stood
on Kafah St. near the Fadl Mosque
not far from where the dates-seller hollered
something to a passerby. Only when she crossed

to the street's other side in her black coat
did I see shadows under her eyes, like those cast
by ancient Babylon's hanging gardens. After that
I heard her knees creak
as she limped through a swarm

of flies near a vendor's
cut-open melon. Maybe
among her ancestors, millennia ago, a temple slave
wandered this very street, hunting
for incense to burn
so the dead rats' stench in the alley where she lived

wouldn't make her retch. Today, seeing
the woman on Kafah St. whose face
is a prophetic mural on a wall
of skin, I wanted
to tell her something, but when our eyes met
she gazed at me contemptuously, as if

it was a sin to peer without permission
into Mesopotamia's last hidden library, her heart. You
were born here and yet she once shunned
you too and withdrew. But it's worse now. With
bombs falling all around, she stands
motionless, stillness the only

vocabulary that counts: each vowel,
the desert growing hotter at midday; each consonant
a once triumphant empire, dead.

MESSAGE FROM A MAN NOT FAR FROM THE SINAK BRIDGE IN BAGHDAD

Hey. Over here. Ignore the bulbul
sitting on the branch above what's left
of this address. Look at
the charred innuendoes on the stone walk
where Hanif's house still stood
last week. And see that burnt vine
near the broken bench
in what was once the garden—it's the line that separates
what we crave from what we can get.

How typical that the wind
blows dust across the blown-up veranda now.
Still, hope never dies. Who knows
what can be built from the rubble?
Maybe a museum of photographs of ideas
dying in makeshift clinics
where the syringes are made
from old soda cans.
Or possibly a billboard promoting
the virtues of bowing before
whoever breaks down your door.

The human spirit is never singular—
some poets flee the city,
others remain, giving voice
to haunted litanies, each extracted
syllable by syllable
from the locusts' vocabularies.

No matter how many corners turned. Or straight stretches
traipsed. Some of us stay
in the *we never left* part of town.
We are its debris, what's left behind. Well-intentioned but
with human flaws, the poets
make of us what they can.

An applied "Poetics of the Usual"

for R. J.

Under the Iraqi date palm, replace
the rocket launcher
with a billboard publicizing Oman's beachfront forts. Or maybe
something more local should be touted—*Visit*

the plain where King Nebuchadnezzar
ate wild grasses and went insane. The bridge
from one thing to another is always
just around the corner. Here

for instance. A child's chubby face. It's burned. Outside
the hospital, screaming in her mother's arms, she is
the epitome of lyrical, wildly shaking

her head side to side as she reinvents, to
a beat made of shrieks
and hoarse raspings,
music's fundamentals. Look at her left cheek's

blistered skin, lighter than a piece of wet cellophane
stuck to a fence post at an industrial dump—see how it
peels off more easily than falsehood
from a newscaster's truth. Don't
worry, though: if you're still

tired of it all, we'll fix your boredom yet. After
you remove the kid's hooded sweater and other garb, rub her
with ancient Babylon's aromatic oils, then
when her screaming fades a bit

spread her legs and play
with her clitoris, so tiny and shy
and seductively demilitarized. It's a tossup then
what she'll remember best in the years ahead: the bomb

that maimed her face or how, entering
her body like it was another piece of land
up for grabs, you cleaved it till it quaked. War
or no war, read about it or don't,
true lyricism starts
when the pain's so bad the mind falls apart

and the only artistic compass you can trust
is one with an arrow pointing toward disgust.

A RESPONSE

for S.S.

I think of you in your den, each day
the strain, the anger, growing greater. How you observe
through your window
Pike Peak's shadow reaching for your throat.
Behind you, the televised building in flames
both is and isn't real
while in the prairie vole's snug burrow under snow
the question of why these wars
don't cease is never broached.

Back in the States for a break, I gaze out
my Mid-Atlantic study window. March rain. A bead
of water dangles from a twig tip.

Like the planet compacting
carbon into diamond, my senses
converge on that twig tip.
If only I could press *it*
into a diamond, I'd cut taboo anthems
on dressing-room mirrors and on any glass eye
I could find. Each note would rise higher
than the towers that caved in
when the planes hit their bullseye.

Wanting to be good, I leave the rain alone,
I obey the maple's dictates.
I surrender to the tide's ins & outs. But spectacles
reliant more on the news video than on

what it supposedly depicts
deplete us. Unknown to us
the process places tripwires in our brains.

Please, if the weapons' fire draws too close
or the flies on the ceiling turn out to be
drones reconning your house
or a detonated building's sparks ignite your hair,
don't blame your made-up sand monkey. Instead, learn to bhangra
until your mind's awake. Then take flight
between the 1's & 0's of the binary codes which shadow us. As a writer
maimed weeks ago by what I spied on the road
to Najaf, the home
of Ali's tomb, all I know is this—
this war enslaves the enemy, and also us.

AT A D.C. ANTIWAR MARCH, SUMAN, AN INDIAN IMMIGRANT, NAVIGATES BETWEEN HERE & THERE

You bring it into the world with you.
— Ray Charles

There she was, on her ass on the sidewalk
in late-March sunlight. Two cops
stood over her on H St., or thought

they did. In her head she eyed rice paddies
east of the Ganpati temple near Hindalga
in Karnataka. One cop mocked, *That*

was a nifty Oscar performance, lady, the way
you fell when I brushed against you.
The other cop looked
away, toward a minuscule patch
of city grass where a crocus would pop up

any day now. Other officers

in perfect formation paraded down the street
toward the crowd, pushing it back
like a bulldozer shoving debris
into a ditch of withheld meanings. Her daughter

and her daughter's baby, both safe
behind her, were part

but not all of why she jumped up now, yelling
at the first cop, *No, you're*

the one who gets the Oscar
for pretending to have balls! So much
came back to her then: British laughter, a Muslim infant

skewered by a Hindu sword in Kanpur in '47, the scent
of pickled mangos in an open jar and the sight
of jute coils piled in the bazaar. From there

to now, youth
to this: the bitter
and the almost-sweet. Marching again
she glimpsed faces everywhere. An Ethiopian stranger
whispered something in her ear. After that

someone else yelled. Then

tightrope-walking the border between
one side of her mind and the other
a single thought kept her going—that at the end
of every billyclub on the street

Baghdad burned. Smoke

rose everywhere. Even
the pigeons couldn't breathe.

I MARCHED WITH THE DEAD

for David Coughlin

Some wore colorful beanies and beat
drums with their hands. A woman
with shaved head walked in front of me. At the juncture
where skull met neck, a tattooed eye
with a black bear reflected in its retina
stared at everyone. I tapped her shoulder, asked, *What's*
the tattoo mean? But
her answer was drowned out by people shrieking rhymed ultimatums.
Far away fish climbed Amazonian trees.

I looked around. Darkening the hair
of those near me, the sun disappeared behind clouds. Huge pictures
of little girls smiling in a desert city were stapled to poles
held high above the crowd by marchers
as distant minarets exploded.
What followed then was an evening there
that was noon here
as we protested on Saturday streets lined with buildings
quieter than morgues.
We clamored at people's windows, pleading for a chance
to break open their chests and save their hearts from their mind's piranhas.

I spotted a dead pigeon near a street drain. Its aliases
were Love Dove and Rat with Wings. Its relatives made nests from the
        world's debris and lived on high ledges or in dirt. Now here was one
dead on the street
while anarchists, wearing black bandannas, danced before a pawnshop
        window.
We don't want . . ! we paraders roared
with frenzied belief like yesterday and the day before.

To my left, perched on a stool on a flatbed truck, a woman played cello
while next to her a man played piano, their duet recreating
the sound of missiles exploding everywhere.
Never stopping, we, the unheard, marched on and on.

Once near where I lived a young woman sprinted onto a bridge walkway
        and jumped to death in the river.
Here, today, a chanter with honeyed tongue raced the length of his final
        sentence, then drowned in the silence at the end.

A few days stopover in Palestine

The Palestinian People

They look at us as if we're impossibles
someone said. He meant that
although targeted for disappearance
they still existed, still knew the taste
of olives and figs. And

(he could have added)

remained as intractable
as thorny broom flowering yellow on a slope. So much
is always going on. Not only

the human interactions, but also
the sweet grass-smell
in the goat's nostrils
in the limestone hills not far

from Jerusalem, west of which
lies nothing some people want to know about. Yet at sunrise
the choice to forget

is no option here. The dead sprawl everywhere. The corpses,
just like the living, impossibles who won't budge. Only
a day or two ago, thumbing

through a book, I read Rashid's outcry
from Tent No. 50 in an unnamed camp—

Teach the wind amnesia so it won't transport to me
the apricots' aroma from my fields!

So much gone. Even the leopard. As
a species, it's decertified. Still, we
proceed. Why not? Near Beersheba now, I stare
at the Negev desert
through the leopard's absent eyes. What

a nation! One fact about it is
it has three types of sand. The disowned
cry out for all of them.

Staccato morning

Rat-a-tat-tat,
how many dead in your lap?
The hillside, pink with rockrose, slopes
upward, not to escape, but just to be.
Far beyond the alley where Haneefa lives,
the ibex's horn, a crescent moon with legs,
climbs to nibble wind between weed stems.
The Jordan River knows none of that.
Rat-a-tat-tat,
the dead pile higher on your lap.

Go anyway

Nine days ago on a rainy morning, she.

Nine days. Unleavened bread. Fear, the tour guide
in the house. Hands claw table. What's outside?
Smash. Door breaks open. Scurrying backwards, she
trips, loses balance. That's the start. Afterwards
down needs no map.

Rainy morning. She remembers
how it. Hand embroidered. The dress
pulled up, high thigh. Rain. This moment's
a ravine. Deep gash. In it
the poisonous Black Calla flower soon will grow, then make
her puke. Something in the uterus? Farewell.

Days come, go. Toddler stuffs bread piece
in bullet hole. Ramallah, a rainy mist. Old
carpenter grabs the dowel's shadow, not
the dowel. In the alley.

A woman from the Jenin camp once said, *We.*
Someone wore nice clothing then, very nice. And in
a secrecy so intensely seen. Memory
within memory within—*In case they*
the Jenin woman also said. A camel
now sways in rain near an oasis. On a certain day
another day recalled. Thighs spasm.

Morning, she. Fists bang charred door.
Somewhere else isn't here. But if only. No time
to hide under table. The pounding
grows louder. Who is the girl you were

to whom this is happening
when your memory goes blank?
The fig tree is the fig tree, nothing else.

Ramallah. Nine days ago on a rainy. The sensual,
different then. Today
soldiers come too. Fingernails claw
cheek, an exegesis. Rain falls
on broken violin on the ground.

No one's allowed, the soldiers say. The bread
in the bullet hole proclaims go anyway.
Someone does, crawls beyond the olive's taste, slithers
toward an alley.

On the street, a tank in front of. Thrown stone
clanks metal. The alley's
entrance. *I'm here!* the crawler blurts. A child
watches the slitherer circumvent the vehicle. In
an apartment down the street, someone dies. What if?

Nine days ago. Rainy morning. Bread.

ANOTHER RETURN

for Ahmed Dahbur, a note after midnight

In the headlights, a heavy rain washes dirt
down the embankment into driveway cracks.
The parked car's engine runs. The overhead lamp
is on.
I don't get out.

Behind the steering wheel, I read your words:
I pursue a black rose growing in my heart
and
I saw a bomb walking on hindlegs
in the capitals of the ebbing Arab tide.

Rain beats the car roof.
Like a refugee's garbled code, the sound
signals hope
but in a language still unborn.

Inside your existence, your friend with a notebook disappears.
Somehow, thousands of miles away, he kisses the back
of my hand, leaving bloody lip prints there.
Children with explosives tied to their bellies
blew up in our mouths months ago
when we spoke on the phone through a translator.

In the rained-on car, I look at my hands.

It doesn't matter
that in our dreams, nothing stolen is returned.
Not one grape to one vine.
Not the robbed sound of feet fleeing in Fakhani and the camps.

Not the smell of stewed vegetables or the home
years ago
in which they were cooked long before knowing got jailed for vagrancy.

Why should it matter? It's only a phase.

Throat sounds that mean nothing now
will one day be words for things
language can't stomach yet.

Two weeks after returning, I visit Rachel in Nevada

Through her rented home's window
sun pounded sandstone west of the Moapa River,
another torrid day.
Nonetheless, she confessed how often, when she closed her eyes, she heard
the wind howling off the frozen bay
through the wallboards as a kid.
The house back east, older than Aaron was, was torn down
by the township two years before his death, then reconstructed
in her head. There, if the kitchen faucet broke, it didn't
matter, just as long as she could listen
in her old room to his stories about the mom
she never knew.
Until he died he lived in the same town, but in
an apartment a mile from the bay.

The desert came natural to her. Heat for her
was nothing but ice's other side.
She practiced singing while scrubbing
whatever needed it
in her house off Rt. 169, an hour
from The Strip.
Wedged like an unbudging chuckwalla between two rocks, her mind
held its place.

No matter what she wanted, this was what she got—
when the dry wind battered the dune primrose's white petals
she felt the flower's seizure, how it convulsed
like a sand rat after getting bit by a rattler
or like John Clark who in 1915 hid under his buggy
to escape the heat.

Hours later, ripping
his shirt to shreds in a dehydrated delirium, he died
in the Mojave a quarter mile from a well.

My first night there, I drove her to work in Vegas.
A tawdry club a few blocks from The Flamingo.
Still, once she stepped on stage, the dive's
mood changed. As focused
as the ancient artist who sketched a flute-player
on a boulder west of the Moapa further north, she had a way when she sang
of distorting notes into a lyricism that set revelation free
like a stiletto blade unlocked with a wrist-flick by an itinerant unwilling to be
       halted by those too frightened to cut deep into where
meaning begins. And so it was. In every song
her blues-exalted voice undulated toward
unearthed reveries. Finally, drained
but undaunted, she ended
the night's last set with "Fever," reinvented—
You give me fever when you cactus me,
fever when you make my love-cave bleed,
fever when your Nazi oven
makes ashes of my needs.
When she concluded, some in the audience
seemed mystified, others went wild.
Our eyes met. She smiled palely. Walked backstage.

After the club closed, before we left
she chatted with Hakim, the piano player, telling him
ghost voices in the cliff dwellings further south
were what she heard as she sang that night, adding—
They take us as far as they can. And then it's up to us.

Even though we're still here

Memory: Late afternoon, Mr. Gallagher, WW2 vet, Feb.1964

Through the window—
whipped by the wind, a leaf
skids across snow
where the railroad tracks swerve

toward Massapequa. He swallows
another rye shot and beer chaser at the bar
while in the back near the jukebox the roadcrew guys
guffaw at

a group joke. Not distracted
by them, he quizzes, *What kind of damage*
does a ticket to Jersey City do to a fella's

wallet these days? The job at Republic Aviation
lost long ago, the anchor tattoo on his forearm
moors him in contaminated waters that

have left him frail. *Dumb slut fucked*
some ordlee then went vamoose, he babbles
about his nurse ex-wife, not mentioning
the split lips and swollen eyes which taught her
to screw elsewhere. Only

in his 50s and he remembers
hardly anything anymore, except
one Coney Island outing
when he bought Brendan
and me, each of us
six years old, all
the candy we could eat although he can't recall another
of the day's components—how

he herded us against our will
onto the Ferris wheel by ourselves, while he guzzled beer
on the boardwalk with other WWII vets
who, like him, told stories without

revealing who they were. At ride's end
when we ran crying toward him
he held our hands so gently that we knew
for the first time how good it felt
to be rescued by a soldier sworn
to protect our lives.

After falling asleep in the chair

for Lily Radner

The llama strolls out of my dream into an actual field
east of Lantana Sq.
where I once panicked and could barely breathe.

Aging bodies creak, trees in the wind. Don't worry
where I am now. All you need to know
is I still exist.

Once as a boy during the Korean war, I imagined
bombs dropping as I crawled in terror through
a mustard-flowered empty lot toward
the carpet mill on Nepperhan Ave., hoping
to find safety there. But no matter how hard I tried
I couldn't reach it.

Another time, a few days before my ninth birthday, a man
with wide-brimmed hat laughed at me in front
of Tony's Groceries, so I ran away. That evening
like many others
my crazy uncles butchered the buffalo-sun on the Palisades.
Blood dripped down dark rock and seeped brightly
into water.
I watched from the river's Yonkers side.

Remembering all this, I think of you, Lily, of how
long ago you taught me that beyond
the cliffs there was fear, yes, but also
grasses taller than any
I'd ever seen before, as well
as so many other things
to listen to and touch.

LINES WRITTEN AT AARON'S GRAVE

Windless nights made him think.
No water lapped sand, no
reeds scraped each other, no
noise at all. And yet.

He didn't believe in silence.
He heard, he swore, *something*.
Silence was itself a sound, he claimed, one
made by all other sounds departing.

For him, a wind that slowed to nothing
was still wind, but differently, just as a thought, fading
as one falls asleep, is still a thought
but reborn as a one-legged loiterer in a dream.

Hearing as much in void
as in sound, Aaron drummed
his thigh with a finger,
never once screwing up the beat.

TWO EXCERPTS FROM AN UNDERGROUND MANUAL FOR AGING VETS

Remember. Down in the last place you squirm into
in the old hotel,
there's no difference between
nerve & bone
& the only thing you can see
is the picture a birdsong makes
in the mind of a man who lives
in a world where for centuries
all the birds have been extinct.

Directions. With a magnifying glass
study the tiny skinflakes
between your toes.
Dig them out & roll them into
one piece between your fingers, then feel
how sticky they get, like a small
ball of putty. Now
dispose of it. This is
step no. 1. After this
do the same on the rest of your body
until you finally comprehend
what it means to start disrobing when
your only clothing is your skin.

Beginning with a single memory, the layers form

for D.S.

It's snowing but not
here, although there's a dirty pile
of it on the night corner now—I can see it
through the open car door just before
you slam it in my face. God
it's cold—and snowing
but someplace else, weeks earlier
at the frozen canal's edge across the street from where
your parents live.
I hate, down a ways, the Whitmore's storm-blurred boathouse
        and the sound
of kids playing hockey on
a stretch of snow-cleared ice. And then
the snow's falling even heavier, blowing
at me from across the canal
and suddenly I'm here, a month
later, you
slamming the car door in my face, yelling
I never want to see you again!
and you don't.

It seems like only yesterday
I was home on vacation. My mother dead
four months by then, I exited
Basil's Poolhall and spotted you
walking by. God
was it cold, the park ponds frozen, your pity
the methadone the addict takes each morning, the snow
wind-flung from
sky and branches and . . . No

snow's falling now, though. Just that dirty pile
on the corner, Broadway and 112th in NYC, the
West End Bar two blocks north, me
about to puke, you
yelling, *I don't. I won't. I.* Ooooh I can still feel it, that moment
doing what all moments do, *pass,*
as you storm away. Drunk, I can barely
see. I am
flesh built on rhythm's bones. No one
wants to teach their kids the truth, that this is how
prophecy begins.

Soon it's a year later, another
winter, I'm on the bus to
the induction center. Little do I know
at that moment that what I know
of pain misdiagnoses what it is. Soon
I won't. Next stop
Fort Gordon. Then. And so it went. Finally
back from war two years later
I want to be the soothsayer who
foretells. But foretells what? Is it possible
to know? It's 25° F
& dropping. A gale, raving shrilly
between buildings, leads me home. Plodding
through a dirty snowpile in the past, I end up
decades later
in the here & now, my
M-16 magazine empty in the middle of a firefight, dead
and wounded bodies strewn everywhere
like a jumble of words in a language
no one understands. Fuckit. In
a more familiar lingo, someone wrote
almost two centuries ago

about sailors who coughed gobs of phlegm into the East River
along the Brooklyn docks as they worked on ships in the riggings or astride
       the spars
while smoke from nearby foundries blackened
their nostrils and tongues.
No historian remembers them now.
Or us either—even though we're still here, almost
eighty now, our stories
at last running out.

Memorial Day

Today I should
say something, show you
ghosts. The ghost
of language first. This syllable
a mirror, this one smoke, a third
a hand movement too quick to see, the fourth
a shell—but where's the pea?
Oh, that's right, there is no pea or for that matter
any shell at all.
The trickery's what's real, nothing else. Or so
the speech-givers screech.
But I'm not one of them. I'm more
a telekinetic email artist, conveying
messages to random places
as I wander through a maze
of Monday barbeques in a locality synonymous
with suburban holy. No matter
what I do, though,
artillery thunder on all sides drives me nuts. Soldiers
& their dying words
sprawl on the ground all around. When
the medics arrive, they lug
everything away on stretchers to a makeshift ICU
on the border between a fact & its validity
while nurses, fussing
over corpses, bless them as
they grow stone cold.
These are the fragmented dead. So many parts
left behind in arbitrary spaces. A foot
in a gulley, a Dear John letter hidden
under a napalmed goat,
someone's swagger

nothing more now than a bloodstain in dirt.
This is why patriots turn away,
why dads get sloshed before firing up their grills,
why everywhere
the ribbons' manic yellow shrieks hysterically *the dead died right.*
And what about this?—an apparition, wielding
an entrenching tool in
a shady corner of an unmown yard, digs
deep into the carotid that leads
to the nation's brain.
To find out where the apparition
came from, follow
the signs pasted to electrical boxes & boarded-up windows
& stapled to utility poles. Soon you'll arrive
at the day's main event. The passing parade. Don't waste any time. Gaze
at the marching bands, the vets in uniform, the mayor
in his open car, the majorettes, their legs
stretched clear to China.
All the while take note
of the costumes & bunting, of how well they cloak
what the spectacle wants no one to know—
that it itself is the lone specter left,
the ghost of beliefs long shown untrue.
Lower your eyes now. Or don't. It's up to you.

TIME

Older, I know
how the wet snow's weight
strains branches.
                    Some snap, others
simply curve so much
they become misshapen.

The snow piles up on branches
like silence in grandma's ears
years ago.
                    One day she hissed, *Us girls*
don't wear hairnets so our brains won't
fall out, but to creep out drunken hands!

Decades later I hear a bird land
on a fence post in the snow. Or is it mist
drifting over river ice? Don't
                                    be so fancy
I tell myself. It's a memory—dad's eyes
closing the final time.

The snowfall's biblical. Each flake
whirls chaotically, a fact in a parable
that won't cohere. Numbed
                                    by the cold
I traipse, head down, into gusts, inching
forward, heading into the whiteout.

One last hike is all I need. One more border
to cross. But the snow's
too wild
                & thick. The wind shrieks

through a Mekong village. Trekking
in deep snow, I fall

exhausted. Under the snow
my fingers find, in the moment's cold confusion,
a coherence. A child's
                    hand among
Ramadi's rubble. The snow's blowing
swirling all around me. Where am I? I don't know where to go.

THREE DAYS AFTER BOMBING SYRIA

I remember spring. How the wind blew
through the magnolia in bloom
ripping off petals & heaving them
in chaotic zigzags to the ground.

Now, not knowing which way to turn,
an uncertain mid-September slows down
until, immobile as stone,
it's alone & seasonless.

Later, south of Corner Ketch Rd.,
I sit in the grass, leaning against
a honey locust trunk.
The trail I hiked here winds on & on.

In the growing dark, a Lenape brave recalls
the mashed cranberry's taste, how it
enlivened the roasted pheasant leg
years before the local marsh disappeared.

The wind dies down,
but where, we ask, does it go?
Our killings began long ago.
The stars are out.

What is it?

What is it that makes us turn our backs as the sun drips blood while it
        hangs from the torture rack?
Under everything that's wrecked, old guards scheme to keep their power
        intact. While in the Middle East
ISIS is in crisis, the US declares itself the nicest.

At home, armies assemble. In the light & in the shadows. Standing
        Rock, Charlottesville, El Paso, Seattle. Long on the horizon, a
        new civil war has begun.
Here is a bee in a bonnet, free land out west, a knee on a neck, a badge
        on a chest, forever & ever the American quest.
And here a crowd parades forward from decades ago, led by a platoon
        of weeping mothers carrying on their shoulders a palanquin on
        which is placed Emmet Till's grotesquely beaten swollen body.
And over there, also from the past, a drum major, leading a column of
        clowns, holds a baton carved from an old whipping post while
        behind him *Yankee Doodle* bellows from an outmoded Victrola as
        government officials give out free cases of coca-cola to the locals.
And here, only recently, a face on a poster, she was run over by a Nazi
        driving an All American car, she wasn't, the driver proclaimed, a
        true citizen but an imposter.

In America the only meaningful size is GARGANTUAN, achieved any-
        way you can— steroids, sugar, implants, piling on military gear.
Weighed down, more weighed down, most weighed down, the nation
        wobbles forward, warring everywhere.
The Republic's waistline exceeds the planet's.
Uncle Sam waddles like a riddle, fat not from substance
but from dining on our distance from it.

Overseas, what digital horse's racing hooves are a desert choir, what
        steed is this with Jesus' head & a mane of fire?
It is *our* steed, the Epitome of Desire, it wants to reduce whatever re-
        sists it to ashes & mire.
Look, the steed bleeds, it is the Christian God naked, dire, a burning
        bush turned into a flaming gyre, the national spirit's destiny
made manifest, its holy fire—

Disguised as the sun, look what comes
to brighten & sanctify America:
the self-styled truest prophet, Isaiah, burning bright & white.
As he rises over us, listen to him prophesy—

Iraq's stony plains Palestine Afghanistan
each in turn
each in turn
must burn
must burn.
Only then can our empire's horses run
wherever they want across these lands.

NIGHTY-NIGHT

Ugly. But snugly. Powdery-winged
it keeps arriving. What kind
of blight or insight rides tiny & headless
on the moth's back in my reading light?
Nighty-night.

The furthest I can journey now
is to the universe's edge,
the eyeball's border. Beyond that's the clinic
mama once shrieked about.

Someone wants to talk. False teeth
are displayed. Mama's stories show up
in somebody else's mouth— daily. Tante
Henka grins idiotically.

Sitting in a corner chair with a knife,
mama's mama's eyes were bright.
Don't get close to me, the old lady told
her butcher husband as he strode toward her.
Cut by her before, he halted.
His face, inscrutable. Hers, scarier.

These days, other bedtime stories are crazy too.
What about Kabul? Basra? Srinagar? Aleppo?
Twinkle, twinkle, little star
me wants to know
what use words are.

WHAT CAN I SAY AND WHY SHOULD I SAY IT EVEN IF I CAN?

voum rooh oh
voum rooh oh

the unsaid, ugly because unsaid, grunts
Mr. Frog clucks like a prince with a speech impediment

why language when
sound of sea battering Owen's head one April is enough
why sound when it's
a lump of cement
why—when der parrot ist dead as doornail in cage
why—when Uzi in suitcase eats whole breadloaf before spying black
          olives in the hand of the waiter riding on a humpback's shoul-
          ders while trapped in the phlegm I cough into the urinal of
          love
why—when woman in the mountains won't come down, won't leave
          that meadow, won't
descend to see me on the plains blowing my eagle bone whistle next to
          a campfire at the edge of a streambed winding under the cradle
          in which an ancient Mesopotamian silversmith's infant sleeps

my friend Cesaire
he watched the maple walk its chest out glaring at the stars in the
          heavens under the snail's foot as the snail crawled toward
          everything that wasn't what it was

aagggh! oowed! xycuth!

why language when language doesn't work
what's the word for rainforest
hidden by one flake of dry ankle skin

under your sock inside the sneaker
that resides in the brain
of another planet's chieftain

what is the word for, how doth one bespeaketh
genitalia that can't be kissed
or
skullbone that won't open so I can pour universes in
or
our freedoms are jigsaw puzzles made from what people's rubble?

language, that Dachau where every meaning is a Jew no longer there
where every gypsy dulcimer player must entertain the guards with tuneless
        solos before choking to death on gas for the Fatherland
where every black must enroll in the local minstrel show before they're al-
        lowed to doze in Hotel Oven for the peace & quiet there. . .
and then . . .
the end

BALLAD OF THE PRODIGAL SON

How yellow the forsythia was,
now how white the snow,
how red the blood in foreign lands,
how fragile what we know.

Ice-patched roads wind for miles,
too cold the February air,
barren snowfields on all sides,
the silence groans *beware.*

Epilogue

SONGS IN SEARCH OF A MAD STREETSINGER

Little songs
carried along,
songs about
north & south,
wild songs hidden
in the head of a singer
who has no mouth

Tiny songs burnt
to a crisp by a star,
psychotic songs
that break the strings
of the lead guitarist's guitar

Songs about snow
songs about rum
songs that make the nightingale
getting shock treatments
begin to hum

Songs for a streetsinger
crippled by fear
that another war
is drawing near

Songs of love
in the midst of the night
when the has-been & demented
grow second sight
as they gnaw pigeon bones in cosmic light

Songs for the river
songs for the moon
songs that gasp & shiver
songs with no
recognizable tune

p. 19—**LZ (Landing Zone)**. During the Vietnam war, a place where aircraft, particularly helicopters, could land.

p. 20—**VC**. Acronym for Viet Cong, the northern based liberation forces against whom the U.S. fought in Vietnam.

p. 22—**APC (Armored Personnel Carrier)**. Military vehicle for transporting troops and equipment in combat zones.

Mekong. A river beginning in the Tibetan plateau and running through China into Vietnam, then through its delta region before emptying into the South China Sea.

p. 23—**Tonkin . . . Gulf of Tonkin Incident**. The Gulf of Tonkin is a body of water between Vietnam and China. On Aug. 2 and Aug. 4, 1964, two alleged unprovoked Vietnamese communist torpedo attacks against the US navy in the Gulf prodded the US Congress to pass, and President Johnson to sign, "The Gulf of Tonkin Resolution." The Resolution signaled the beginning of what became known in the US as the Vietnam War.

Unfortunately, these attacks, as described by Washington, were a mixture of manipulated facts and outright distortion.

The first attack, against the *USS Maddox*, a destroyer, did indeed happen. However, although supposedly not on a military mission, the *USS Maddox* was in fact intercepting North Vietnamese radio communications, then relaying that information to South Vietnamese troops for the purpose of helping them launch raids against the insurgents. Additionally, although it was true that Vietnamese torpedo boats fired on the destroyer, what Washington failed to mention was that the *USS Maddox* fired *first*, which meant the insurgents weren't the aggressors but the attacked.

The supposed second attack occurred on a night of heavy thunderstorms, a roiled sea and dense squalls. In the midst of this turbulence, some of the *USS Maddox's* crew heard noises and saw unidentified light which they interpreted as signs of an attack. Other crew members, however, weren't sure. The ship's Captain, for instance, after experiencing an initial disorientation, concluded the ship wasn't under attack. In spite of this, the White House decided to declare it to be an attack.

Eventually, the U.S. Naval Institute determined that "the evidence suggests a disturbing and deliberate attempt by Secretary of Defense McNamara to distort the evidence and mislead Congress."

For more information, see: *"The Truth about Tonkin." 2008. U.S. Naval Institute. February 2008. https://www.usni.org/magazines/naval-history-magazine/2008/february/truth-about-tonkin.*

p. 35—**Taíno**. Puerto Rico's indigenous inhabitants. Also indigenous to the rest of the Caribbean.

p. 36—**French plantation**. Vietnam was a French colony before the U.S. took over the west's war against the Vietnamese freedom struggle. During French rule, one of the main colonial exports was rubber. Rubber plantations made fortunes for many western companies and individuals.

p. 43—**Victor Charlie**. Grunt slang for Viet Cong.

p. 46—**Está loco, hermanita**. Eng: "He's crazy, sister!" The word *crazy* is meant affectionately here, as in "full of life."

p. 59—**Quenépa** is a small round Puerto Rican fruit with sweetish but also citrusy taste. Sometimes compared to a lime.

p. 60—**Mi querida hermanita**. Eng: A tender way of saying, "My dear little sister."

p. 61—**Tan dónde están usted, Elesio, heh?** Eng: "So where are you, Elesio, heh?"

p. 81—**Sometimes/I disperse Allah's tiny parables just to show Him I can** is based on Sura 2, Verse 26 of the *Qur'an*, which says, "Behold! Allah doesn't hesitate to use a gnat or mosquito, or even a more lowly insect, as a parable."

p. 83—**Kaaba**. A building inside Mecca's Masjid al-Haram or Great Mosque. The Kaaba houses a black rock considered holy by Muslims who believe the rock was given by God as a sacred sign to Adam and Eve or, according to a different version of the story, to Abraham.

p.95—**Diné** (*dĭ'nĕ'*)). The name by which the Navajo prefer to be called.

p. 96—**He winced at the bite of the dogs the police used to chase him down** is based on Walt Whitman's "I am the hounded slave, I wince at the bite of the dogs" from "Song of Myself," section 33.
Tumbling walls buried me in their debris is a quote from Walt Whitman's "Song of Myself," section 33.

p. 110—**To Yasin Taha Hafiz** was inspired by "Woman," a poem by the Iraqi poet named in the title.

p. 117—**Bhangra.** Punjab folk dance originally associated with harvest festivals. In the later 20th century, however, it evolved, through Indian immigrant communities in other countries, into a type of club dance that integrated traditional Bhangra instruments and movements (acrobatic jumps, body twists and thrusts) with other influences—hip-hop, pop, disco, etc.

p. 118—**Karnataka.** One of India's 29 states, located in the southern part of the nation.
       Hindalga. Indian village near Karnataka's northern border.

p. 125—**They look at us as if we're impossibles** is modeled on a line from "The Impossible," a poem by Palestinian poet Tawfiq Zayyad.
Teach the wind amnesia so it won't transport to me/the apricots' aroma from my fields! is a quote from Palestinian poet Rashied Hussein's poem "Tent Number 50."

p. 130—**I pursue a black rose growing in my heart** . . . and . . . **I saw a bomb walking on hindlegs in the capitals of the ebbing Arab tide** are quotes from the poem "In Memory of 'Izziddin Al-Qalaq" by Palestinian poet Ahmed Dahbur.

Acknowledgments

I WANT TO THANK Jenny Drai, a poet and author of, among other books, *The History Worker* and *Wine Dark*. Her feedback after reading an early draft of *Nightmares* was enormously useful in prodding me to tighten certain poems and rethink some of my phraseology in others. I can't thank her enough for her role in helping me to strengthen the book.

Another person to whom I owe much thanks is Theresa Wisner of the Bartow Trust. Because of her persistence and belief in *Nightmares*, she did everything in her power to help me secure the Trust's permission to use the image I wanted for my cover—Native American artist Rick Bartow's drawing, "Things You Know But Cannot Explain," a work impacted by his PTSD.

While writing *Nightmares* I'd had no contact with Lawrence Siddal for almost fifty years, yet I knew I had to thank him here for the role he played as my post-army psychotherapist. For five years, he inched me toward understanding my anxieties rather than instinctively running from them. This not only increased my self-awareness—of my anger, contradictions, what was behind them, etc.—it made me more alert to the pain in others' lives. Thank you, Lawrence Siddal.

I want to thank, too, Spuyten Duyvil's staff and editors for supporting the book. They did this at a difficult time in my life, when I was starting a months-long recovery from major surgery. Especially to be thanked is Aurelia Lavallee who patiently answered all my questions and led me step by step through the pre-publication process. One couldn't ask for a more ideal work partner.

Additionally to be thanked for their support during the writing of *Nightmares* are my family. They have been a source of strength for me not only because of their love, but also because in general their ideas, anecdotes and—yes!—disagreements with me helped me to remember the importance of seeing the world, as much as possible, *as it is*. Thus, I thank my son Nikos Arjun Bohm, my daughter, Adriana Leela Bohm, my son-in-law, Shane Jackson, and my grandchildren—Che Jackson, Rana Jackson, Anand Bohm, Baylee Fee and Cole Bohm.

My final thank you goes to those publications that previously published a number of the book's poems, sometimes in altered form. A list follows.

"While listening to Sun Ra, the spirit momentarily stirs" (*3 A.M. Magazine*)

"Another Return" (*Abalone Moon*)

"Time" (*Consequence Magazine*)

"Beyond the sentimental," "Written for someone today," "Moments: dusk to night" (*Counterpunch*)

"When it doesn't come together except in nightmares" (*Dead Drunk Dublin*)

"I see it," "Uday al-Bakhir talks spontaneously in Tompkins Square Park," "Intersecting angles," "To Yasin Taha Hafiz," "Message from the man near Synak Bridge," "An applied Poetics of the Usual," "A response," "At a D.C. antiwar march, Suman, an Indian immigrant, navigates between here & there," "I marched with the dead" (*MiPOesias*)

"Memorial Day" (*Radius: From the Center to the Edge*)

Born in Queens, NY in Aug. 1943, Robert Bohm is a poet, cultural analyst and Vietnam Era Veteran.

After his 1966 college graduation, Bohm, an aspiring writer, was drafted into the army in early January 1967. Although by then he'd been influenced by Beat Generation nonconformity and had developed a cynical attitude toward the war, it didn't occur to him to publicly resist it. In spite of his sense of alienation, he knew little about the growing number of antiwar protests and, although he supported the civil rights movement in principle, he never thought of joining it. Political activism wasn't his thing. Therefore, it was no surprise that, when drafted, he reported for duty as ordered.

Following basic training, he served at the US Army 225th Station Hospital in Munich, Germany as the facility's Census Clerk in the Registrar's Office. The job required him to visit the hospital's wards daily to track their status—number of beds filled, new admissions, discharges, etc. While doing so, he often spoke with patients and sometimes got to know them.

Although the 225th didn't specialize in treating the wounded from Vietnam, it did have such patients. Not directly from the war, however. Instead, they were vets currently stationed at US bases in Germany. A portion of these patients suffered from supposedly healed injuries that, having flared up again, required further physical therapy or surgery. Others were admitted for psychological reasons—insomnia, disorientation, erratic behavior, depression and other symptoms.

Of those with psychological problems, Bohm discovered that although many were quiet, others liked to talk, at times eagerly. When he had time, therefore, he conversed with them. But he found it difficult. Their often disjointed tales frequently included unnerving descriptions of things they couldn't forget . . . A grenade-inflicted open belly wound. Or a nightmare about going insane. Or the memory of a little girl standing terrorized in monsoon rain before a ruined hut.

As the months passed, back home the nation became increasingly embroiled in heated debates about political and cultural issues—the war, Black Power, feminism, the counterculture, the nature of democracy, what being a "good" American meant. Inevitably, these debates were echoed in the military. As Bohm participated in them, he spontaneously identified with those voices directed against society's exploitive power structures. Consequently, he began thinking about patients' combat stories as not merely anxiety-producing, but also as informative. For him, they provided an alternate view of these men's situation than the one he'd heard from many career officers and noncoms—that these patients were fakers, the inference being that they weren't "real" soldiers but whiners attempting to con their doctors into giving them a medical discharge. Rejecting this notion, Bohm came to see these men as not only enduring authentic war-related mental distress, but also torment from the slander that they were phonies looking for a coward's way out of the service.

From Bohm's perspective, the military hierarchy benefitted from this view in two ways. First, it allowed them to continue promoting the idea that good soldiers personify a type of heroic manliness that never gives in to fear or any other form of emotional breakdown, whereas those who fail in this regard are useless. Second, given that the war was controversial at home, the military leadership saw no reason to supply the public with another messy fact about the war (i.e., the number of US troops suffering combat-linked mental damage) that antiwar protesters could use to belittle the armed forces. Rather than take this risk, they chose to scapegoat the psychologically wounded as weak and unpatriotic self-servers looking out only for themselves.

Eventually, fed up, Bohm wrote a memo to the facility's leadership, accusing them, among other things, of downplaying Vietnam vets' war-connected psychological problems, then of complicating those problems by ridiculing their stories.

The content of Bohm's memo was ignored. But he himself wasn't. He was ordered to undergo three months of psychiatric treatment.

This conflict between Bohm and the military was a prelude to his life-long activism, not only in regard to US wars and their unacknowledged impacts, but also in regard to other justice struggles. It also signaled his direction as a poet—to find poetry where it's not supposed to be found: among the othered, the scapegoated, the oppressed.

Meanwhile, at the 225th Bohm's interests concerned more than politics. One such interest was Suman Kirloskar from India. Living in Germany on a visitor's work visa, she was a clerk in the hospital's Registrar Division where Bohm also worked. After meeting, she and Bohm became friends, then eventually romantically involved. Months afterwards, they married and soon started preparing for life after the army. They decided he would get an MFA degree. He chose UMass and was accepted.

Discharged in late Dec. 1968, Bohm started classes that winter and received his degree in 1971.

A quick synopsis of his life since then is as follows.

For nine years after earning his degree, Bohm worked various jobs while pursuing his writing. First, he taught at Karnataka University in India, then Springfield College in Massachusetts. Subsequently, he secured a position as a foster care worker, from which he eventually resigned to return to India in 1977 for three-quarters of a year. While there, he drafted what would later become his nonfiction book, *Notes on India* (Boston: South End Press, 1983), which critiqued the west's lingering colonial views of the subcontinent. Then, following his return to the US., he taught at the Che-Lumumba Elementary School in Amherst. Concurrently, he completed his first full-length poetry volume, *In the Americas* (Sunderland: Panache Press, 1979). The following year it won the GLCA (Great Lakes Colleges Association) award for best poetry book by a new writer.

At this point (1980), Bohm left New England and his previous job history behind to become a freelance writer outside of Philadelphia in Wilmington, DE. From then on, he's worked primarily as a ghost writer of social justice articles, reports, policy papers, speeches, etc. for various grassroots organizations and movements. Simultaneously, he's written poetry volumes and essays under his own name.

Although throughout their fifty-five years of marriage the Bohms' primary residence has been the US, they've lived in and visited India many times over the decades. They have two children, a daughter and son, and five grandchildren.

www.ingramcontent.com/pod-product-compliance
Lightning Source LLC
Chambersburg PA
CBHW031526120626
46545CB00005B/2015